22 Steps To Success
Your Guide to a Fulfilling Life

By Krysta Gibson

Success is yours!

Blessings,

Krysta

ISBN: 978-1-4303-1218-5

The author may be contacted at:
krysta@krystagibson.com
www.krystagibson.com

Also by Krysta Gibson:

The Entrepreneur's Toolbox:
How to Succeed In Your Small Business
While ManifestingYour Destiny

Comments on Leading the Spiritual Life

Embrace Your Day, Love Your Life CD Program

**Go to www.krystagibson.com
for information about these titles.**

Acknowledgements

*M*ost authors say their book would not have been written without the help of certain people. This is true for me as well. What is different for me, though, is that I don't know the names of most of the people I want to thank because they are the over 40,000 people who read the newspapers *The New Times* and *New Spirit Journal.*

Many of these people have written, called, and emailed to let me know that my writing has helped them lead happier lives. Because the newspapers are free, I have no way of knowing who these people are unless they get in touch with me.

I think the most humbling experience for me was the time I was boarding an airplane at the Seattle airport and the flight attendant who took my ticket said, "Thanks for your articles, Krysta, I love to read them!" I have no idea who she was and probably never will. It was fun to see the faces of the other passengers as they wondered who I was!

To all my readers: thanks for being there. Thanks for letting me know that the words I put on paper have been helpful to you. As I said in my first book *Comments on Leading the Spiritual Life*, a writer without readers is like a river without water. Thank you for being the water that brings my river to life.

Thanks to all the advertisers, and others, who have supported these free newspapers over the years. A free newspaper doesn't last very long without advertisers and others believing in it and being willing to be involved. Special thanks to:

Tess Sterling at Stargazers; Susan McGinnis and Marilyn Scheer at East West Bookshop; Hriman McGilloway with the Ananda Center for Self-realization; Paul Martin at Stonehouse Bookstore; Brenda Michaels and Rob Spears of Conscious Talk Radio; Dr. Pat Bacilli of the Dr. Pat Show; Christine Upchurch and the Reconnection; Lori Aletha of the NW Psychic Institute; Iona Sharron; the Maitreya Center; Libby Kresky, Ph.d.; Judith Campanaro; Richard Dupuis; Rev. Alia Aurami; Kim Miller; Starfeather; Rev. Richard Levy and Maureen Levy; Nancy Macdonald; Debbie Fortman; Jean Hendrickson;

Audrey Smith; John Skyrman; Mike Carlson; Will Tilse; Linda Baker; Jan Havlisch; Stacey Gauthier; George Phelps; Janet Hickox; Mantanya; Louise Hay; James Wanless.

I would also like to acknowledge:

the Builders of the Adytum, Paul Foster Case, and Ann Davies for the marvelous spiritual training program they provide. It is their studies in the tarot that provided the impetus for me to write about the 22 steps or keys in this book.

Ernest Holmes, Catherine Ponder, Joel Goldsmith, John and Jan Price of the Quartus Foundation, Wayne Dyer, Lester Levenson and Larry Crane for all of their writings and recordings which have served as foundation stones on my path.

Frances Gibson Howell and Laurence Gibson, Sr.; Michael Lou Gibson; Kitti and Reverend Eugene Lindusky; Agnes Pauro; Archie Dicksion: treasured family members who have been there for me in one way or another over the years.

Margot Montel-Westover, my massage practitioner who helps keep my energy flowing and open while also being one of my most loyal cheerleaders.

Martha Norwalk and John Jennings for their long-term support of my work and for the most delightful dinners at the Sailfish Restaurant in Monroe.

Larrisa Thomis, my releasing partner extraordinaire: yes!

Blue Jasmine Rose (Jazz) and Rhododendron Celeste (Rhodie), our Cardigan Welsh corgis who bring such sweetness and mischievousness to my life: how could anyone think about living without the joy and happiness you bring me every day?

Finally, a special thanks to Rhonda Dicksion, my partner, book designer, co-publisher, editor, #1 Cheerleader, and laughing companion. We work hard but we also know how to play hard. Thanks for being in my life!

To anyone not mentioned, please accept my thanks and my apologies for not listing you; it was an innocent oversight. Consider yourself thanked!

Krysta Gibson
Washington State, August, 2007

Table of Contents

KYRSTA GIBSON

Preface

Ask anyone and they will tell you that they want to be successful at something. Maybe it is a relationship, a career, sport, hobby, or spiritual practice of some sort. We humans seem to be wired for success.

People's definitions of success vary, of course. For some, success means having lots of money, a big house, the latest car and technological devices. Other people see success as feelings of inner peace and being able to reach deep places during meditation. Still others feel successful as long as they are not failing at something! Just getting by is a lot for some people to accomplish!

Woven into the fabric of everyone's life are threads that can be used to make life exciting, happy, prosperous, and successful no matter what sort of challenge we might be facing.

We humans can be complex creatures with different tendencies, habits, and preferences. But at the core of our beings, we are the same – much as some people might prefer to negate that piece of information.

The 22 Steps to Success are based upon ancient knowledge that has been passed down through many generations and in many different traditions. Each step is actually an aspect of ourselves, an archetype if you will. Some people are familiar with these archetypes as the major arcana of the tarot.

If the word tarot conjures up images of an old woman, shawl around her head and neck, seated at a darkened table in a musty room I ask you to discard that image. I invite you to make room for a new image, one of the tarot as being a book of wisdom, a book which contains the sort of information that can support you in becoming the person you want to be.

Briefly, the tarot is a set of 78 cards which contain symbols that can be used for divination. On a much larger scale, the tarot is a spiritual map that can lead us deeper into ourselves and which can give us guidance for our daily lives. The first 22 cards in the deck are known as the major arcana and this book is loosely based on some of the meanings of these 22 cards. Each of these meanings carries a lesson that I call a step to success. I am not going to get into the history of the tarot because that is written about so eloquently in other places. It makes for some fascinating reading, so I suggest you Google "History of Tarot" if you want to pursue this further.

If all this talk about the tarot has you ready to run away, let me say that you don't need to know anything about the tarot to use this book. In fact, you don't even have to care about the tarot. You can even think it is a bunch of hooey or be afraid of it.

Basically, this book was written by focusing on each card and then writing about an aspect of the meaning of that card, an aspect that would be helpful to people in living successful daily lives.

Aficionados of tarot will find that I reference the name of the card being written about in each chapter, but I do so in a hidden way. This is just a little bit of extra fun for those who might enjoy it.

Let's get started, then, along our road to success.

1
Beginnings

"Beginnings" are filled with excitement, freshness and the mystery of unknown factors. The beginning of anything is also a time of risk-taking, a bit of danger and the expenditure of lots of energy. Keeping in mind that every day of our lives is a beginning, how can we approach such times so we maximize their potential?

Whether we are starting a business or our day, each beginning is also an ending. Something must end for something else to begin. Sometimes this is not very evident, but if we look closely we always must give up - or end - one thing to begin another. Entering into partnership or marriage with a lover we give up, or end, our single days; beginning a business, we let go of the security of paychecks from an employer; as we began our day this morning we let go of yesterday. We also, however, bring with us everything from our collective past as we begin any journey. Everything which has gone on before in this lifetime and others, is carried with us as we move forward.

Both of these aspects can be very positive and can be used by us to make beginnings happier and more successful. Bringing this to the level of our every day beginnings, we do not have to be bound by our yesterdays while at the same time we can bring forward into today all of our accumulated wisdom and knowledge from the past. So if, for instance, we have been depressed, unhappy, thinking gloomy thoughts, we do not have to keep doing that today if we don't want to. If because of our thinking and feeling, we have been attracting unhappy circumstances, today we can change our thoughts, change our feelings. We can end the old behavior and start afresh right here and right now, today. This is one of those simple ideas which is very profound but, because of its simplicity, most people miss the profundity!

Let me expand on this idea a bit. Because a beginning of any kind involves letting go or ending of prior situations, this is a time when we can make enormous changes in how we want to live our lives. Although we bring our past with us at the time of a beginning, we do not have to be bound by it. On the everyday level this means we do not have to be bound by our past. This means that, at any point in time, we can decide to begin anew, turn our ship around and go in another direction. Simply turning the ship around does not put us immediately at our new destination; it does, however, point us in a new direction.

In terms of making changes in our lives, what this means is that on any given day when we have our beginning, which really happens all day not just in the morning, we can change the way our life is going if we want to do so. Who is to stop us from declaring a beginning any time we wish? Who is to say that if we are tired of being unhappy, stressed out, poor and miserable, we cannot turn our ship in another direction? Turning our ship around will probably involve some effort on our part as will keeping it going in the new direction, but if we want to do it, we can.

We take our past with us wherever we go. This statement usually has a ring of negativity to it. I think it can be very positive. No matter what our past may be, we can draw on it to help us. What I mean by this is much more than "we can learn from our past mistakes." Although that statement is true, I think it is also very limiting. Our past is more than simply events which took place at a time gone by. We are the sum total of our past. It is encoded into our very cells, into our beingness. As we step into our future, we carry with us an enormously useful ally, our past. Sometimes our past is painful and requires the healing of unconditional love before it can serve us. Sometimes our past is one of success and completion and it serves us as a blueprint for further success and happiness. Ignoring our past, acting as if we are not carrying it with us, is like trying to walk with a ball and chain tied to our ankles, pretending it isn't there. It is far better to pick the ball up and take it with us.

Whether we are beginning a project, our day or a lifetime, there is an "us" who sees the big picture of what has happened, is happening and will happen.

Some people call this our Higher Self, others like to use the term Spirit or Beingness. No matter the label, it is who we really are, it is the aspect of our consciousness who is in touch with the Source of all which exists, the aspect of us who channels to the Earth plane all the high-powered energy we can ever use. Aligning ourselves with this inner Self at our beginnings places us in a position of wholeness and centeredness that allows us to receive from the Life Source/Force Itself. Traveling our path in conscious union with our Spirit/Soul, as our Spirit/Soul, starts the journey off with a positive cosmic bang!

Many times our beginnings feel like we are walking off a cliff with no visible support or assistance. Our minds start telling us all the reasons why we shouldn't be doing what we are, warning us of the many dangers and pitfalls of our chosen path. Fear can set in followed quickly by paralysis. It can feel very foolish to go ahead with our plans anyway, to have total faith in our guidance, to know that even though we may fall into a great abyss, not only will we be okay, we will thrive.

We must remember that those of us who choose to follow a spiritual path won't always live our lives in such a way that others will understand what we are doing or why. Our actions will not always be condoned or supported by those close to us or by strangers either. It takes great courage to live by inner standards, to follow our feelings and intuition when doing so is not popular. But if we want popular, perhaps we should choose a different path.

Each moment of our lives can be a new beginning no matter what our circumstances might be. Each moment can be a journey into ourselves, into life itself. Despite whatever pain or suffering we may have experienced in the past or may suffer in the future, our lives can be ones of deep joy and love. Life lived in conscious union with our Higher Self/Spirit/Beingness is one of ever present adventure, sparkling newness, and expanded awareness.

Declare your beginning now and see what happens!

KYRSTA GIBSON

2
Manifestation

We are manifesters, every one of us. We, and everything around us, exist for the express purpose of manifesting Spirit in form. We may not always like the way we manifest or what we manifest, but to deny that this is what we do is to deny the world we live in.

When most people hear about manifesting, they think in terms of things or money – manifesting a new car or a bigger salary. Although we certainly manifest in those ways, there is a more basic and all-encompassing way in which we are manifesters. We are channels for Spirit to experience Itself in form doing whatever it is we do with our lives, whether we are making money or baking bread. Remembering this - that we are channels for energy rather than the originators of it - puts life in a totally different perspective. Our job is to direct the flow of energy and use it for constructive purposes. To do this we have been given certain tools to work with: our minds, wills, emotions and bodies – in other words, our personalities.

Mind

Using our minds, we discern and decide where we will focus the energy. On an everyday level, we decide what career we will follow, what kind of car we want to drive, who we want to have for friends and so on. Throughout our lives we work with the power of the mind but only rarely do any of us use it to its full capacity. With our minds we create images and dreams, some of which manifest in material form and some of which do not. Whether we are trying to manifest an emotional healing, a state of exalted spiritual ecstasy or a Rolls Royce, the clearer and more vividly we can focus our mind the greater our chances of accomplishing our goal.

Our minds are very powerful tools that we tend not to develop to their potential. Most of us waste our mind-power by allowing ourselves to think each and every thought that passes by in the psychic atmosphere rather than by being conscious choosers of what thoughts we will and won't entertain. Some people don't even believe they have the power to choose their thoughts and allow themselves to be used as a host for parasitic thoughtforms and then wonder why their lives are such a mess.

Will

It is by engaging our wills that we use our minds to focus on what we want to manifest in our lives and in our worlds. The will seems to be one of the more difficult aspects of human nature to discuss as it gets confused with outer imposed limitations and disciplines. Will is that part of us that we can use to keep our minds and emotions on track. We use our mind to choose and to focus; we use our wills to keep our minds where we want them to be. Perhaps a good analogy might be a train and railroad track. Our lives are the train, we are the engineers and the tracks are our wills.

How many times do we decide to do something, get clear on our goals and then at the first sign of hardship, abandon our efforts? Engaging the will, the part of us that can gently but firmly keep us on track, makes the difference between manifesting or not. I am not talking about will power. When we are doing what we want to do, when we are clearly following our right path, we do not need will power which usually means forcing ourselves to do something we don't want to do. Will is softer, a gentle nudge to keep us going when it would be easier to stop.

Emotion

Thank goodness our emotions are finally beginning to get some good press within spiritual circles. We seem to be leaving the dark ages of spiritual thought which saw the emotions as bad and in need of total sublimation. We are beginning to accept the idea that having and expressing our emotions is not only healthy but spiritual as well! In manifesting, emotions play a very important part in two ways. First, our feelings can give us clues along the way as to whether or not we are on course. Secondly, we can use our emotions to create an atmosphere around us that will help us manifest what we want.

Emotions are an excellent barometer for us to check our progress. When we don't feel right about something or someone, when we are miserable or angry all of the time, our emotions are trying to tell us something about where we are, who we are with and what we are doing. Paying attention to our feelings and releasing them can be an enormous help in living a happier life.

Creating our personal atmosphere occurs because of the use of our minds and wills as well as our emotions. The emotions can be so powerful in this regard we would be cheating ourselves not to use them. Depending on what area of manifesting we are working with, we can use our emotions to create atmospheres of safety, sacredness, healing, prosperity, health, wisdom, humor or any other feeling we wish to embody. We have the power to generate the feelings that correspond to whatever it is we wish to manifest.

Try it. You know what it feels like to be very safe, to feel secure and fearless. Close your eyes, relax and remember how it felt when this was true for you in the past. Let yourself feel it in every cell of your body. Stay with the feeling until you sense it enveloping you from within you. Allow yourself to continue generating this feeling while opening your eyes.

By generating the feelings that accompany whatever it is we wish to manifest, we will attract it to ourselves much, much faster and more accurately. This is why prosperity teachers such as Catherine Ponder tell us to dress and act as if we already are prosperous when we are developing our prosperity consciousness. Dressing and acting in prosperous ways helps us to feel prosperous which helps us to become that way.

This fact that our emotional bodies are so powerful is the reason why healing our emotional aches and pains is vital to the manifesting process. If we are carrying deep wounds with us that have not been attended to, our personal atmospheres will broadcast hurt, pain and hardship. It is difficult, if not impossible, to manifest happy circumstances when we are broadcasting misery.

Body

Without our bodies we would not be effective on the earth plane of existence. In manifesting, our bodies are crucial since they house the spirit, mind, will and emotions. It is through our bodies that we can move and act, which we need to do if we wish to manifest on the material plane. One of the areas in which so many of us fail is in that of action. We hope, pray, visualize and affirm… but don't step foot outside the front door! Using the example of finding one's right livelihood, a New Thought minister I once knew used to say that one should be clear on what one wants, visualize it, use spiritual mind treatment and affirmations – then, apply to jobs in the newspaper, send one's resume out to businesses, etc. Simply because we are using "spiritual" means to manifest something is no reason not to use the world of matter to accomplish our aims. It's funny. We want to create on the physical plane but want to do it by only acting on the spiritual plane! Of course, that is a huge misunderstanding since matter is spirit in form. Working at the level of matter is only working with Spirit in a different form than when we work with Spirit in our minds or at other levels of consciousness.

Spirit

As humans, we tend to identify ourselves with our minds or our emotions or our bodies as if they are who we are – rather than seeing them as part of who we are, as tools for us to lovingly use. The hardest thing for us to understand is that we are Spirit/Soul in form. We are in form for various reasons not the least of which is to learn how to navigate in the world of matter. By continuously and deliberately aligning ourselves with/as Spirit we can learn how to use our tools to co-create and manifest as was intended by our Creator.

Manifesting on the earth plane may not always be as easy as waving a magician's wand, but it does not have to be gruesome hard labor all the time either. When we align ourselves with our own more expansive aspects of consciousness, our Beingness, and allow this to be our guide – when we actually allow this part of who we are run the show – manifesting (which is synonymous with life) can actually be fun!

3
The Subconscious

*T*here is probably no one within the human potential field who would deny the power of the subconscious mind. Yet we frequently act as if we do not have a subconscious or that it holds little power for us in our daily lives. The exact opposite, of course, is true. In fact, I am beginning to wonder just how great – or small – a part our conscious minds play at all!

Our subconscious (or "deeper" mind) is our connecting link with that part of ourselves some call Soul, others call their Higher Self, or an expression I like, Beingness. The subconscious is a literal storehouse of data about ourselves and the mass consciousness. It is our creative aspect of mind as well, setting about to create whatever it is told to create without question or judgment. It is just as happy creating sickness as health since it cannot discern between them. It is mysterious, silent, potent and can be our biggest ally or greatest enemy depending on how we relate to it.

If we want to know what program our subconscious is working with all we have to do is look at our lives. Whatever we are experiencing in our reality is what the subconscious believes. Some of the programs we decode will make us happy, and then there will be those that cause a big sigh. There are few, if any, people who can say they are 100 percent happy with what is being created in their lives. Fortunately, the subconscious is very open to suggestion and to change. If we do not like what we are producing, we can change it.

Most of us are familiar with techniques to alter the content of the subconscious: affirmations, visualizations, and hypnosis are among the more common and effective. Also very effective are therapeutic relationships such as support groups or individual counseling, and bodywork which works with subconscious programming held in the body. Each of these is only intermittent feeding of information and programming to the subconscious and, though valuable, somewhat limited in what each can accomplish.

The most important information we give to our deeper mind is the ongoing data it receives moment to moment as we go about our daily living. If the information we give to the subconscious all day long contradicts what we tell it during a morning affirmation period, guess which programming wins! We can use subliminal tapes, written messages to ourselves or shout it to the roof tops, but if we then live in contradiction to what we say we want the subconscious to produce, we may as well save our breath and our time.

We were programmed slowly in the first place through the day in and day out existence we had as children. To think that can be changed by saying affirmations once a day while we reinforce the old beliefs through our lifestyle is only joking with ourselves.

Whatever we wish to produce in our lives we need to use a multiple approach for the best results. Yes, use of all the techniques I mentioned above is great, but then let's take it a step further.

Watch your words! Listen to yourself during the day. Does what you say about your life and yourself jive with the affirmations you did this morning? If not, take a deep breath the next time you start to berate yourself or talk about how sick or poor you are. Our words have power not only due to the principle of vibration on this planet but also because our subconscious is listening all of the time, awaiting its instructions. It pays close attention to what we say.

Watch your actions! Act in accord with what you say you want in your life. Every time we move, we are making an imprint on the cells in our body. We can either continue the old imprints that we say we are trying to change or we can constantly be making new ones in accord with what we truly want. If, for instance, you are trying to improve your financial condition, you must act as prosperous as possible. Spend money joyfully as if your bank account were full to overflowing. I'm not talking about spending money foolishly. I'm talking about attitude. Act as if money is not an issue and your subconscious will begin to create that circumstance for you. It may take some time, but it will happen.

Watch your thinking! This should go without saying since we know how powerful our thoughts are and since they feed directly into deeper mind. But, how often have you prayed, meditated or affirmed your higher good only to think when finished, "I wonder if that worked?" Talk about using a cosmic eraser! Reprogramming the subconscious mind involves paying attention to our thoughts, weeding out those in contradiction to the new reality we want accepted by deeper mind. Some of the thoughts we have will require healing. Most simply need to be escorted to the trash bin.

Watch your environment! Are you busy affirming health, happiness and prosperity and then surrounding yourself with nutrition-poor foods, complaining friends and unkempt clothing and housing? Your subconscious mind is affected by the environment and by the people you choose to associate with. Make your environment match your new reality as closely as possible and it will materialize much, much sooner.

I like to think of my subconscious as a High Priestess of olden days whom the people saw as their intermediary with God/ess. She is that part of me which intercedes between my conscious and superconscious aspects of mind as well as with all of creation. I hold her in great respect recognizing her immense power. Perhaps this is where traditional religion came up with the idea of the people needing Priests or Priestesses to intercede with the Deity: it is a watered-down version of our inner Priests and Priestesses whom we are constantly calling into action. Each of us was ordained at birth and given our ministry in this world. Our altar is daily life; our thoughts, words and deeds are our liturgy. The only salvation we need is from our own ignorance of just how powerful we are as integrated, whole beings.

KYRSTA GIBSON

4
Creativity

One of the reasons our society is so commercialized and materialistic is the fact that so few of us use our creativity and powers of imagination. The vast majority of people work at jobs they do not like in order to make enough money to pay the bills for things they must have in order to keep the empty part of themselves from bellowing out in pain. One bumper sticker I have seen says it well, "I owe! I owe! So off to work I go." Cute, but a tragedy.

The irony is that whether we use our powers of creative imagination consciously or unconsciously, they work! So, even people who are absolutely miserable with the boredom in their lives are actually being creative without knowing it – they are creating boredom. The trick is to use our powers as consciously as we can for chosen results rather than unconsciously imposed ones.

Sometimes it's easy to feel stuck with our lives, to feel that we do not have any choices about what happens. Although this may appear to be true, what is also true is that we are actually very powerful creative beings and always have choices – even when our choice is to accept what is. No one else can do that for us or to us.

In order to allow ourselves to begin to feel our creative nature it is helpful to spend some time just contemplating planet earth. As humans we are part of this planet and share some of its qualities and attributes. The first thing to notice is how incredibly vast and diverse this planet is. Then notice how unbelievably abundant she is. Pay attention to her cycles of creativity, destruction and rest.

Our Vastness and Diversity

When it comes to our creativity we have been gifted with both vastness and diversity. Most of us don't use even a tiny bit of our creativity. We live one day the same as the one which went before, not questioning our ability to make changes, only complaining about the sameness. Our imaginations are able to think with profound diversity when we allow them some freedom. We limit what the imagination can do for us while it is actually unlimited.

Begin to spend some time every day daydreaming. Yes, we were taught that this is a waste of time because we aren't doing anything. Hah! Daydreaming is one of our most fertile activities. From it flows our future! Anything any of us has ever done occurred in our minds before it happened in the world of matter.

Who would you be and what would you do if you could be or do anything, if you had no limitations and no one to stop you? What is your heart's desire? What does it look like? Feel like? Taste like? Smell like? What pops into your mind when you put it in neutral? Problems and challenges? Ask them to wait outside for awhile, this is your time for daydreaming, not problem solving.

When you allow yourself to do this exercise, you may notice an interesting thing. Whatever you find yourself imagining as a possibility a voice inside your head offfers at least one reason why it won't work or why you shouldn't do it! You may find yourself caught up in a delightful reverie of life as you would like it to be only to awaken with the uncomfortable thought, "But, it will never happen…" I ask, "Who says and why not?" It already did happen in your mind. Daydreaming is a real event; what we daydream has already happened. The question is: do we want to allow it to occur on the material plane as well as the daydreaming one?

This simple process of having some daily daydreaming time will open your heart and your mind to a level of personal creativity you would never have experienced otherwise.

Our Abundance

Like our Mother planet, we are blessed with abundance especially in the creativity department. Our bodies, which are extensions of our hearts, minds and souls, are composed of billions of cells that are constantly rejuvenating themselves! It has been said that every seven years we actually have an entirely new body, that our cells replace themselves on a seven-year cycle. The really good news is that they know how to do it without any conscious input from us. I think that's pretty spectacular. This means that the body you live in is so abundantly creative that it knows how to continuously maintain and recreate itself.

Because we live in our bodies, or at least try to, we are very close to our own creative abundance at every moment. By consciously aligning ourselves with our innate bodily abundance we can increase our creativity in other areas of our lives.

Our Cycles

When some people think of creativity they think they must be creative at all times or else they just aren't being creative at all. This is not true. If we look around us we see that there are at least three cycles to creativity. One is the creation part, another is the destruction cycle, the third is the fallow period.

Nothing exists without something else having to be destroyed. Many people don't like to acknowledge this aspect of creation since they feel it is a negative viewpoint. A good way to understand this is through the analogy of moving your household. In order to move from one location to another, it is necessary for you to tear down your current household, put it into boxes and move it to the new home. Without destroying your old home, you cannot have the new one. The same thing is true of the food we eat. It cannot be used as fuel for our bodies without being destroyed. A tomato is actually destroyed and ceases to exist as a tomato in order to become part of our bodies.

In order to create something new in our lives, we must be willing and able to tear down the old, to let it go, in order to move into our new creation, whatever it may be. Lots of times it is even necessary to tear down the old before we know where our new home is. This can be scary, but if we approach it with a sense of adventure, it can also be exciting.

A critical aspect of creativity is the allowing of rest periods. We all know that land needs a rest from having crops planted, trees take a break between dropping all their leaves and growing new ones, bears hibernate. We can't expect ourselves to be constantly creative in a productive sense. We need our breaks and can learn to see such rest periods as necessary parts of the creative process.

Add creativity to your daily life

One of the best ways to add zest and excitement to our lives is to allow our innate creative natures some room to express themselves. One does not need to be a trained artisan to be creative. Find a way to consciously create something every day. Remember you are doing this for yourself, not to sell at a craft fair!

Write a poem. Draw a picture of how you feel or of how you want to feel. Take needle and thread and make a pouch for one of your stones. Get out the crayolas and color a picture in a coloring book. Take some modeling clay, play dough or potter's clay and make a small bowl, statue or piece of abstract art. Write in your journal. Sing a song. Bake bread. Plant seeds. Give a speech to your stuffed animals.

All of these are ways for us to be creative, to encourage that part of ourselves to come out and play. Making a point to spend some creative time on a daily basis will make a tremendous change in one's life in short order. Once the Universe sees we are receptive to our creativity, the ideas and feelings begin to flow freely. Then we can begin to consciously apply them to areas of our lives that require our attention.

It's our Empire

My life is my Empire and I am Empress. The same is true for you. Certainly we co-exist with other people and certainly we co-create with God/dess. But, each of us has been given dominion over our personal space and world. We have been given all the tools we need to allow God/dess' innate creativity to move freely through us and out into the world around us. It is our decision whether or not we thwart these basic urges or allow them room to be expressed. Our decision makes the difference between a life well lived with a sense of personal satisfaction or one thrown away on the trivialities of this world's existence.

5
Order

$\mathcal{A}$ well-ordered life is usually a more peaceful and harmonious one than is a life that is cluttered and in disarray. As is frequently the case, this statement seems to be true on several different levels – physical, emotional and spiritual.

No one would argue that it is much easier to work at a desk that is well organized than to work at one which is piled high with debris. But, even those piled high with debris will work if the debris is organized!

Few will argue with the idea that a well-ordered emotional life, one in which past hurts and pains have been dealt with, one in which some regularity of expression exists, will provide a person with a better basis for happiness than will one which is not.

When it comes to one's spirituality, however, there seems to be no real sense or order at all. Rather, many of us seem to take a very random approach to our inner lives without giving ourselves any sense of structure or order. Is it any wonder, then, that we hear cries of "This stuff doesn't work!" It can't if we don't. And we can't if we have not given ourselves some sort of ordered plan to follow which is implemented by our intellectual processes.

Unfortunately, spiritual seekers are sometimes portrayed as a group of weak and "woo-woo" nitwits who run hither and yon without any logical rhyme or reason to our actions. Someone says that they heard a particular time period is a prime one for certain activities and off we charge without even checking out the source of the information. In most cases it doesn't matter anyway, no harm will be done whichever way we decide to act, and potential good may actually come of our actions. But, in some instances in our life it matters very much how we apply our intellect if we wish to succeed.

My belief in the intuitive part of our natures is very strong. In fact, I live my life based on my intuition and inner knowingness. However, to live one's life based strictly on intuition without also applying the gifts of reason and intellect is silly and only leads to chaos, not order. Unfortunately, this seems to occur with great regularity in the lives of many people. An intuitive flash is received and the recipient does not bother to check the source (is the information coming from inner knowingness or personality desires?), but pushes actively ahead before making ordered decisions based on tangible life circumstances. By applying our natural gifts of reason and intellect to create order in our lives, we can avoid the potential embarrassment of the Emperor who found himself unclothed!

How can we apply some order and rationale to our lives? The initial step seems simple and is simple – we do, however, tend to want to make it complicated! In any area to which we wish to apply order, we ask ourselves, "What am I trying to accomplish?" Yes, yes, I know, this can seem to be the hardest part of applying order, finding out what we want, where we are going! But if we would spend a bit more time on this first step, we'd find the others much easier. Whether we are rearranging furniture in our living room, changing careers or deciding to follow a new spiritual path, we must first gather information and make a decision about what we want to accomplish.

Second, we ask ourselves, "Is my current situation structured to support what I want or will it sabotage my efforts?" We may have the greatest ideas in the world as to how our living room would look, but if a wall is standing where we need to have a doorway, we have to look at the feasibility of our plans… or be willing to put a door in. So it is with the rest of our lives. If we find that our current life structures – work, relationships, attitudes, habits, health – do not support and complement what we want to do, we must be willing to either change what we want or modify our structures so that they are supportive of our desires.

In terms of one's spiritual process, we can ask questions such as: have we imposed some sort of plan or process or practices on ourselves? Have we determined where we want to go in our spiritual life? Is the way we are living now supportive of that goal? Are we meditating, reading spiritual literature, spending our time and resources toward this goal? If not, do we need to modify our goal or do we need to change some of the structure in our lives?

Lastly, the best order and reason in the world can be applied when we remain flexible. Always allowing ourselves room for modifications, expansion or contraction of activities and goals is vital. We cannot foresee all things. We cannot know in advance how anything in our lives will work out despite our best efforts to know. Remaining flexible in our attitudes and in our structures affords us the best opportunity to continue growing. Being willing to change one's goals when one discovers another route would be more advantageous is the mark of an adventurous and open soul. Flexibility allows us to take advantage of true inner guidance when it arrives. Sometimes we need to transplant our tender baby shoots to a new location where there is more sunshine and rain. If we have put our roots down too deeply, we may not survive the relocation.

Life is filled with options in all areas. We literally stand in front of a smorgasbord of choices. Despite some protestations to the contrary, no one else can come along and put their choice of food on our plate. We alone control what we accept or do not accept into our minds and our lives. We can decide to choose carefully and knowingly, balancing to create a healthy input or we can run down the line and throw any sort of available food onto our plates and end up with indigestion.

It is not difficult to take the time for ourselves to make careful choices about how we wish to live our lives. Such choices are based on how we feel about ourselves and on how much we value the life process we are experiencing. As each moment passes it will never return to us again. It seems to me that applying sound, reasonable and logical order to our lives will only benefit us and help us make solid decisions as we move along. And staying open in our choices will allow us to benefit from the delightful unexpected events and opportunities which come our way daily if we watch for them.

Living one's life from a spiritual perspective can be exciting, refreshing and anything but boring. Let's add order and reason to it so that it can also be Divinely sane.

KYRSTA GIBSON

6
Intuition

*U*nfortunately, of the many changes and beginnings that are started by well meaning people, many of them will be casualties. Why? There are lots of different reasons why we fail (and I use that term loosely since I don't believe in failure – only a change in plans) on a program of change or growth that we set for ourselves. But I believe that the single greatest reason is that we do not get in touch with and follow our inner guidance, our intuition. We look outside ourselves for the right program or method, of which there are many available, without first turning inside to see what we need to make the changes or to begin the project in question, indeed to find out if the changes we want to make are in line with our life purpose at this time. By accessing and using the vast amount of information at our disposal, we increase the chances of success immeasurably.

Inside each of us dwells a very wise woman, wise man, a Hierophant and Sage who has access to the secrets of the Universe. This Wise One inside of us is us as Soul or Beingness. It is the us who knows why we are here on earth, what we need to learn in order to grow and develop, what the plan for our lives is. Yet, how often do we take counsel with our inner Wise One, how frequently do we ask this One for guidance and information about our lives? Probably not often enough! Most likely we turn to other wise people around us before we think of turning to the one closest to ourselves, us. The truth is that those we deem wise are so because they have tuned in to their inner source of wisdom, not simply because of books they have read or courses they have taken. The wisdom we seek is as close as our own beings; we don't even have to leave home to find it!

We can observe that the plants and animals around us have an innate knowledge of who they are. When we plant a rose bush we don't get lilies! On a cellular level the rose bush knows it is a rose bush and proceeds to become one. Cats know they are cats from the time of kittenhood and wouldn't dream of trying to bark. I believe we humans also have an innate knowingness of who and what we are. By contacting our cellular imprinting and allowing it to lead us through life, we can grow in phenomenal ways not possible when we struggle and push ourselves to be what we are not.

Tuning in to our Wise One requires receptivity, discernment, trust, solitude, silence, commitment and the willingness to experiment and take risks.

If we don't pick up the receiver of a ringing telephone, we won't be able to hear the person on the other end of the line. And if we don't engage our inner receiver, we won't be able to hear the voice of our Wise One. The inner Voice does not shout nor does it insist that we listen. It very politely awaits our receptivity to it before beginning to share its wisdom. Being receptive means being willing to hear what the Voice wants to tell us and this is not always easy since the information will not consistently please us at the level of our personalities! If we think our inner wisdom is telling us how wonderful and perfect we are, what horses to bet on and the ten best ways to become rich and famous, we'd better listen again. We aren't hearing Inner Wisdom, we're hearing our own human desires. To truly engage ourselves at this deep level, we must be willing to put aside our own thoughts, our own desires, our own plans and be open to totally new information.

Discerning between our Wise One and our own ego or some lesser entity outside ourselves, is learned with practice. For me, I have found that my Wise One seems to communicate without a lot of fanfare or hoopla, and is not accompanied by strong emotions but is quiet and very clear. There is a sense of solidity to the information and not infrequently I will have to stretch my limits in order to use the information (that translates into: it frequently means I have to do things I'd rather not do or quit doing things I like to do!). And when I have tuned in to something of great magnitude for my life purpose, the information is usually accompanied by what feels like an electrical charge or tingling throughout my body. On the other hand, ego information is usually accompanied by fear and anxiety or by euphoria, depending on the situation. Rather than a sense of knowingness it offers a very unsettled feeling.

The way I came to make these discernments about the information I receive was by being committed to contacting my own wisdom and because of a willingness to experiment and to take risks. If we want to contact our Wise Ones we must be committed to the process required of us. Being into it one day and not the next will garner only scattered and very unreliable results. Either we want to live from a deeper part of ourselves or we don't. This does not mean we will do so perfectly, but it does mean we are committed to trying and won't be swayed off-track the first time things get a little difficult.

The best way I know to validate one's guidance is to take the risk of following it and see what happens. I believe the process is very much one of trial and error, first in smaller areas of our lives, then moving progressively to more major ones. The way I talked myself into being willing to take the risks, especially when the information seemed out in left field, was to remind myself that simply following the ego had not fared me so well in life. Even making big mistakes with following inner guidance couldn't make things any worse and the potential for vast improvements was certainly enticing!

If we aren't willing to provide ourselves with some places of silence and solitude in our lives, it will be very hard to hear anything from our Inner Teacher. Although I am certainly referring here to outer silence and solitude, spending quiet time in contemplation and receptivity to ourselves, I am also referring to inner silence and solitude. This means quieting the mind, the thoughts, giving it all up, placing our wants, desires, visions, dreams and hopes on hold long enough for other impressions to surface into our consciousness. It also means letting go of other people's expectations and demands. I like to call this "inner solitude" – getting all those other people out of my head so I can be alone with myself!

Learning to trust ourselves and the information we receive is a must for this process to work. We must believe and trust that we even have an inner Wise One to contact. We must trust that there are deeper parts of ourselves. The only way I know of to establish such trust is to spend some time going as deeply inward as possible until we have an experience which convinces us.

Anything else remains hearsay and not worth trusting.

Each of us has an inner partner, teacher, holy one, therapist and counselor in whatever we want to be or do in life. So often we seek the outer partners, teachers, etc. and then are grossly disappointed when they fail us in some way. We have a 100% guarantee from our inner Wise One who is willing and able to provide us with anything we ask. Perhaps we won't always like what we are given. Perhaps we will become impatient with the timetable used by our inner teacher. Perhaps we will be tempted to think our outer selves are really the wiser ones. But consistent effort prudently applied to contacting and using our intuition will pay off.

Whatever your next step is, even if it is deciding what your next step is, put contacting and using your intuition at the top of your list. Spend some time developing this skill and applying it to whatever project you find yourself engaged in. Whether one is beginning a weight loss program or opening a business, placing trust in the Wise One within cannot fail to be of enormous help.

7
Love

Every year we celebrate February as love month. All around us are red hearts, cupids with bows and arrows and the ever-present message that love is the greatest thing we can ever hope to experience. And, of course, this is true. Love is the reason we exist. Love is our existence. Yet, we see people all around us whose lives are devoid of love; we might even feel we are one of them. If our culture places such a high value on love, why don't we see more of it expressed?

As a society we are scared of love. Yes, I know. We say what we want is love. And everywhere we look people are apparently trying to find love. But, from where I sit, it is very clear how much fear we bring to our search. Why, I wonder, is this so? How can we fear the one thing that we know will make us happy?

The vast majority of us have never experienced love and we tend to fear what we do not know. All our lives, of course, we have been told that we are experiencing love ("But, honey, I am only doing this because I love you!"), when in fact we are experiencing control of our lives by another person. We have renamed control, need, manipulation and loneliness and called them love. No wonder we fear it!

I am probably the tenth million person to say we can't find love outside of ourselves, that if we don't love ourselves, we can't possibly love or be loved by another person. And, it's true.

In my experience, learning to love one's self is an ongoing process of integration. Of course, the truth is we are already whole and complete right now. What we really need to do is recognize our wholeness. We integrate who and what we are to the point that we are recognizable to ourselves!

Metaphysics 101 teaches a profound truth which many of us promptly dismiss. All brands of metaphysics teach that we are comprised of three levels of consciousness: our ordinary awareness or self-consciousness; the hidden depths of ourselves, the subconscious; and the elusive, much sought after, Higher Self or Superconsciousness. I believe we experience true self-love when we have integrated these parts of ourselves so they work together as the unit they really are. The vast majority of spiritual training and teaching has this union as its goal.

The more we become integrated beings, the more powerful we become because love is power. In our world we have become confused about power since what we usually experience as power isn't that at all. Just like love, power has been misappropriated to behaviors that have nothing at all to do with true power.

How do we become more loving to ourselves and others? How do we step into our own center of power and live from that place of integration?

We must remember that being in our power, in our love, is a process and we grow into it bit by bit. I am not familiar with any loving person who started out that way or who became so overnight. Experiencing our own integration is a gradual process requiring desire and effort as well as generous portions of grace from our Higher Self.
Becoming the loving and powerful persons we truly are is a three-step process.

First, we must make the commitment to integrating ourselves. This means we must have the willingness to experience ourselves at all levels of who we are – not just the pretty parts. It means being willing to dive into our subconscious and swim with whatever we find there, accepting it as part of us. It does not, however, mean we must keep what we find!

Second, we agree to live with these different parts of ourselves. We promise not to continue to deny, hide, wall ourselves away from, the different aspects of ourselves. This is a lifetime task. By living with ourselves we can decide which aspects we want to keep and nurture and which we wish to dissolve and return to the cosmic ocean.

Third, we agree to wed ourselves! We hold our own personal commitment service and marry our triad of Lovers. The self-conscious, subconscious and the superconscious join so that they operate as a unit rather than as a group of competitors. Acting from this state of self-unity allows us to be very loving and powerful beings because we return to our natural state. We cease fighting ourselves and we love instead.

Because of this ongoing process, we frequently repeat the above steps and we don't always do them in the same order. But once we begin this journey, the positive results are almost immediate. Although we do not become spiritual giants overnight, we do begin, step by step, to move in that direction. A by-product is a wonderful sense of rightness about ourselves and the world we choose to live in. No, of course we aren't perfected beings. Yes, of course we still have our issues to handle. But now we are doing it from a place of growing integration rather than as fragmented beings who aren't sure who we are or where we're headed.

This is living in the state of love. And when we are experiencing this feeling of internal rightness we begin to overflow it to others in our experience. They feel loved by us and respond in kind. We feel powerful in the true sense of that word, not as a desperate attempt to control our outer world because we are so out of control internally.

Now is a perfect time to begin to focus on our internal selves, to allow them their place in our daily lives, to blend with ourselves and step into our world of personal love and power.

KYRSTA GIBSON

8
Speaking

Our human ability to speak, to make verbal sounds, is one of our most precious gifts. Through this natural endowment, we are able to communicate with one another, carry on complex conversations, ask questions, give answers, sing, express our emotions using sound and direct the course of our lives. Yes, direct the course of our lives.

Our gift of speech is far more than simply a tool of communication. It is a tool for creative works. Through the power of the spoken word we can enhance our life experiences or draw to ourselves great sorrows and hardships. Most people do not have any idea just how powerful the spoken word truly is. If they did, the world would be a much quieter place with people being more careful about what words they let slip into the atmosphere.

Anyone who has studied any metaphysics at all has already heard about this power of articulation. But, how many of us put it into daily use for our own good and the good of those around us?

Words give great power to our thoughts. As we speak, we set into motion vibrations which move away from us out into the universe. Everything is made of vibration, some fast, some slow, but everything is constantly moving and vibrating. When we speak we send out our own personal vibratory message that, because of the way the Universe is set up, must return to us in some manner. The more energy we put into our words, the faster and more concrete the return. The less energy we place behind the words, the slower and less concrete the return.

One of the quickest ways I know to make changes in one's experience is to pay close attention to the thoughts we entertain on a constant basis, especially to the thoughts we verbalize. Of its own, thought is creative whether or not we speak the thoughts out loud. But, once we make our declaration of intent by speaking our thoughts, the creative potential is heightened. Some people don't believe this. They think that the words we say are fairly innocuous. And if those people are not working on uplifting and cleansing their consciousness it is true that the return is so slow and so warped that it may appear their words hold no power.

However, those of us who are working with our consciousness cannot afford the luxury of sloppy thinking or speaking! The more we hone our abilities to focus thought for creative purposes, the faster and more clearly do our thoughts and words produce results. Working with thought can be compared to a knife. A knife cuts easily or poorly depending on how sharp it is. The sharper the knife, the quicker the cut. And the knife is just as happy cutting through an apple as it is cutting through our fingers – it does not know the difference.

This is also true of our consistent thoughts and words. The higher our vibratory rate, the sharper our knife is; the returns of negative thinking and speaking are much faster and accurate for a person who has raised their energetic vibration than for a person whose energies are fairly dense. If you don't believe this, spend some time paying attention to your life and that of your spiritually-oriented friends in comparison with those not actively on the spiritual path. No wonder we sometimes feel like we're riding in race cars!

Just about everyone will admit that, as humans, we are in the process of becoming. None of us is a completed product; we are constantly changing. Because our words are filled with creative power, this means that we can influence our growth by the words we choose to speak – and not speak. When we speak well of ourselves and others, we set into motion positive energies which will return bearing gifts of peace and happiness. When we degrade ourselves or speak poorly of others, we sound out the blueprint for misery.

It is commonplace in our society to gossip, to talk about people in their absence, to carry tales about others which are, hopefully, juicy enough to gain the attention of our listeners! Gossiping, telling and listening, is probably one of the most harmful things we can do to ourselves. It slows down our progress tremendously. The next time you are tempted to repeat gossip you have heard, ask yourself, "Is repeating this tidbit of gossip worth slowing down my spiritual progress? Which do I want more – my inner growth or to feel important because I carried some gossip to others?"

The next time you are subjected to gossip from other people, ask yourself if listening to what they have to say means more to you than your soul growth. If you choose your soul, politely change the subject or leave the situation gracefully. It is not necessary to give the other person a lecture about gossiping; they will understand your message because gossip doesn't feel good to them either.

If the power of our own spoken words can affect our lives, is it not possible that the spoken words of others can affect us as well? Yes, of course they can – and profoundly. Besides watching our own words we will do well to pay attention to what we allow ourselves to listen to. Think about it. Would you allow a friend of yours to walk into your living room with a big bag of their garbage and let them dump it out in the middle of your carpet? I doubt it. Yet, we let others say whatever they will when in our presence because we don't want to "hurt their feelings." If people are bringing their garbage over to our house instead of taking it to the dump we have every right to insist they not do so whether it is physical or metaphysical garbage.

What about jokes? Frequently, people will say something derogatory about themselves and add "I'm only joking – my subconscious mind knows the difference." Maybe and maybe not. It is true that if we send a message to our subconscious and then want to cancel it, we are capable of doing so. But, what about all the times we don't bother to cancel the order we've placed? The subconscious does not know the difference between the truth and a joke. Your subconscious controls your bodily functions, doesn't it?

Think about someone eating a beautiful yellow, luscious lemon. Watch them take a big bite of the lemon. What is your mouth doing right now? Can't you taste the lemon? That's your subconscious working. It doesn't know that you aren't eating a lemon right now. If it can't tell the difference between eating a lemon and thinking about eating a lemon, how is it supposed to know when you're joking and when you're not?

A much overlooked aspect of the power of the spoken word is silence. We seem to think we have to be chattering away all the time and don't leave a lot of room for inner quiet to develop. It is during times of solitude that we will be able to hear messages from ourselves and the quiet whispering of inner guidance. It really is okay to spend some quiet time at least once a day, and for the brave of heart, several times daily. When we restrict external sounds, we open up the space where we can hear the wind, rain, snow, plants, birds and angels speak to us.

Am I advocating that we all become a bunch of boring pollyannas who speak softly and nicely, no matter what? That we hide our anger, our doubts, fears, sorrows behind a plethora of phony sounding words of power? Hardly. We must be real with ourselves. There is no point in keeping our emotions in check, never speaking an angry word when we are seething inside, not allowing ourselves to cry when we feel grief and sorrow, not expressing and releasing our fears and doubts. I believe it is absolutely mandatory to walking the spiritual path that we allow our emotions to move through us rather than collecting inside of us until they explode or make us sick. But, this can be done in such a way that we make it very clear to our subconscious that we're not placing an order for it to carry out. In fact, if we make it an ongoing practice to keep ourselves as clear emotionally as possible, the message to the subconscious is one of clarity and depth. It will get the message that we majestically ride as driver of our chariot, flowing with life rather than hanging onto the side of the chariot in constant fear of falling off!

As we meditate and pray on a daily basis and make consistent efforts to evolve and grow into the best self possible, we will find it easier and easier to speak only the best words we know. We will find, also, that our words carry greater and greater power as we send them out into the cosmos.

When I first began my metaphysical studies, a very wise statement was made to me. "Never say anything you do not want to see materialized in your life." This is a wonderful gauge by which to measure the words we speak and listen to.

As we spin the webs of our lives we have a very potent ally in the form of our ability to speak and be silent. Certainly it is true that we co-exist with many folks on this planet and cannot orchestrate our lives as if we are in a vacuum. However, it is also true that we have at our disposal a virtually untapped power, one that we use constantly, all day long. Does it not make sense that focusing a bit (or a lot) of energy in this direction, in making conscious choices of what words we speak and don't speak, could make a tremendous difference in the quality of our lives. We have been given the ability to make such choices. Let's begin to use it wisely.

KYRSTA GIBSON

9
Courage

It takes tremendous courage to follow one's vision regardless of the consequences. Most of us do not consciously have this degree of developed strength and are willing to forego a set course of action at any signs of difficulty. The good news is that we do have access to incredible strength within ourselves and can use conscious efforts to evolve our latent heroic dispositions!

Courage evidences itself through persistence, concentrated effort, faith, joyful risk-taking and a relaxed sense of humor about it all! It is easy for us to confuse being strong with being overbearing, pushy and ruthless. Our society encourages this confusion by generally presenting strong people as very aggressive and determined to win at all costs to themselves or others. This, of course, is not true. Some of the strongest people I know are soft-spoken unless raising their voice is necessary and they are flexible and willing to change their course of action if it seems called for. Strong people are also usually very gentle people; because they are secure in themselves it is not necessary for them to use physical force or emotional manipulations.

A test most of us are given is that of being willing to persist with a course of action when it seems not to be working or when the going gets tough. Many of us give up way too soon in whatever we're doing and then bemoan the fact that our project didn't work out. Yes, there are times when we are simply off course and change tactics or projects; but, more often than not we are being given an opportunity to develop inner strength and persistence.

It can be enlightening to compare life with athletics. Can you imagine a runner working out for a month and then giving up because she couldn't run a two-minute mile? Yet, that is exactly what many of us do. We decide to try a

meditation technique and when, at the end of a month, we aren't living in
bliss 24 hours a day give it up saying it didn't work. Or we decide to offer our
services to other people in the community and when we don't have a thriving
business in a few months decide to stop.

I believe we can develop persistence by practicing faith. If we truly believe
in ourselves and if we believe that we are being internally guided by something
much greater than our personality selves, "keeping on keeping on" becomes
much easier. We aren't alone in this grand charade called "life on the earth
plane!" We have all the help we possibly need as long as we are willing to ask
for it and to receive it. Believing this at the depths of one's being makes persisting with a course of action we feel is right much, much easier.

Another mistaken notion we have been fed about strong people is that
they never ask for help and rarely accept it when it is offered. Nothing could
be further from the truth. Strong people know they need help from others,
that they cannot do anything of much importance by themselves. Strong folks
have the knack of knowing when they need help and then satisfying that need.
When we feel help is called for all we need do is ask for it. We can call on
friends, professionals, support groups, business consultants, angels, guides,
even nature herself. Of course, it is also true that the strong do not rely on
others to do what must be done by themselves. It is definitely an issue of balance.

When we are willing to be persistent, are operating from a deep faith in
life itself and are willing and able to request help as the need arises, taking
risks becomes a much more joyful prospect. Certainly our fears will pay a visit
anytime risk-taking is on our agenda; but, when we are operating from a place
of courage, the fears tend to walk beside us in formation rather than tromping
all over us!

The best way I know to become accomplished at risk-taking is to start
doing it. The more we are willing to do the things we find frightening, the less
they will scare us. And the longer we sit on the couch chewing our fingernails,
afraid to leave the comfort of our drawn curtains, not fully involving ourselves
in our own evolutionary process, the larger our fears tend to grow. Faced with

courage and love, they eventually dissipate as we stand there chuckling wondering why we made such a fuss in the first place!

One of the greatest signs of a strong person is the ability to focus one's attention and use concentrated effort to attain a goal. It takes practice to train our minds to focus on one thing to the exclusion of all else. Many people have this as a well-developed skill in certain recreational areas such as TV watching! But it's another matter when it comes to applying one's attention to such mundane matters as soul growth or a business proposition that will help other people!

As with risk-taking, we learn to focus our attention by doing it. It is an acquired skill. A good way to begin is to set aside as little as five minutes with the intention of focusing our energies on one goal only. A key to being able to do this is to be sure, before we start a project, that this is what we really want to do. It is most difficult to focus attention on something we perceive to be worthless. This does not mean we never do unpleasant tasks. No matter our goal there will always be some aspects we find easier to focus on than others. But, if we are invested in our overall process, even the disagreeable duties will warrant our concentration.

Humor is one of life's most precious gifts. Retaining a sense of humor about ourselves and about life in general is healthy and enables one to be strong in the face of opposition, discouragement or even apparent failure. Remembering to see the humorous side of everything stands one in very good stead whether the project is one of spiritual practice or cleaning out closets. When we become so immersed in ourselves and our personal drama that we can't remember to laugh and have a good time, we have probably reached the point where some kind of major emotional surgery is called for! And if that's what we need, let's get it.

What if we feel we are a truly strong person, that we are really courageous but nothing we do is working. We are in pain emotionally, physically, financially and spiritually. We feel we have been consistent and focused, that we are really listening to our inner guidance and still life is not working. Sit down in the middle of the floor and wail. Release everything you are feeling. Let it go.

Surrender to life. Surrender to the great Isness with which we are constantly
surrounded and penetrated. Wait for an answer, for some type of movement
from within yourself. It may not come in the first five minutes; you may have
to have patience. But, it will come. Then have the courage to follow the guidance you receive – no matter what it is, simply do it.

You see, despite the less than wonderful things many of us were taught
about ourselves growing up, the truth is that we are innately very noble, strong
and beautiful creations. We are simply in the process of discovering these
truths about ourselves and our fellow travelers. By deeply desiring to express
our highest potential, we set into motion all that is necessary to accomplish
our lofty goal. Yes, expressing our highest natures also means digging down
into our dark murkiness sometimes; we must be prepared for the nightfall as
well as joyfully greeting the dawn.

When we are willing to totally surrender ourselves, at all levels, to the life
force which generates each and every breath we breathe, we begin to live our
lives for the first time. As the life force courses through our veins, we find that,
instead of simply blood, what moves through us is the mystery of life itself.
Through surrender to this mystery we find not only the courage to live a
majestic and eloquent life, but the means of doing so.

10
Beingness

*T*he longer I walk the spiritual path and the more different traditions I investigate, the clearer the picture is becoming that the goal I am seeking is to be myself. Simple though this may sound, it seems to be the ultimate in spiritual achievement. In fact, nothing else matters outside of this.

Sounds kind of dreary, doesn't it? I mean, don't you usually think of spiritual giants as having overcome who they are? As having transformed their humanity? As these very mystical beings who can control the elements, perform miracles and impress the rest of us with their deep spiritual knowledge and understanding? Sounds pretty impressive to me. But, no, I don't think any of these things are the true goal of the spiritual seeker. I think these are by-products that some God/dess-realized souls have manifested for their own reasons. These are optional to the curriculum, not required coursework.

Being who we truly are, though, really isn't the easy process we initially think it to be. If it's so easy why does it take many incarnations to do it? But just because it is not easy, doesn't mean it has to be complicated. I am beginning to see that it is actually very simple – just not easy.

From my current level of understanding, I think we must begin our journey to being ourselves through realizing that we are much more than just the personality self we are so used to seeing ourselves as. Words get difficult here, but we have different aspects or layers of who we are. The personality self, in my case Krysta Gibson, is only the outer shell that I have chosen to wear this time around. Behind that, under it, supporting it, is my core self which gets called by lots of different names – the Higher Self, Beingness, True Self, etc.

The primary mistake that I think most of us make at this point is to think less of our personality or "lower self" than we do of this sometimes hard to locate "higher" self. The tendency then is to denigrate our everyday selves while focusing on the loftiness of the "higher" self we can't seem to contact. No wonder it can seem confusing!

The joke is that we are this higher self/soul/true self/core self! And whatever we find on our plate at any given time is the way and means that this part of us is using to make itself more prominent in our consciousness. It is the way we are choosing to grow and learn, to reintegrate on a conscious level the truth of who we are.

If we can begin to look on our personality selves as the means we are using to express in the physical world rather than as all of who we are, we will have made an enormous step forward. Now, if we can also realize that this true self or beingness is as close to us as our own breath we will have taken the next huge step forward. We will be on the road to becoming who we really are.

There seems to be a tendency within spiritual circles to put down the personality self because it is seen as less than our soul selves. I disagree with this concept because I believe there is no real separation between the two! It is only an apparent one we must learn to deal with effectively. In fact, I think one of the best ways to encourage our conscious connection with our "Higher Self" is to be very nice to our "Lower Self!"

Anyone who has done any form of inner dialogue work – inner child, parent, critical self, wise woman/man, etc. – will relate well to this: just as we can consciously assume a parental role with our inner child so can and does our Soul-self assume a loving leadership role with our personality selves. It doesn't mean we are several different people (although at times it can certainly feel like it!). It means we are multilayered, multi-faceted, multi-dimensional, beings. And once we begin to know this and live it, i.e., be ourselves, we are well on the road to spiritual attainment!

This true self has never lost sight of who she/he is. It has never become totally enmeshed with the earth plane. It is within us and is ever ready to shine a light so we can see where we are going on the rugged pathways of life. It is very quiet, hermit-like, keeping to itself until we beckon it to step forward into our lives. When we allow this soul-self to actively influence us, when we welcome it consciously into our lives, hold on, for all manner of miracles really do begin to happen as anyone who has had a spiritual awakening can attest.

Here are three things a person can do to assist with this inner alignment. There are many others, but I have found these to be of great help.

First, be kind to yourself. Let's treat ourselves as if we believed we really are divinely radiant beings, friends to the angels and inheritors of the kingdom. This means to erase the negative tapes which chant how bad, poor, selfish, ungrateful, stupid, ugly – fill in your own blanks – we are. This sort of internal dialogue has no place in the thinking of a God/dess-realized being so why hang on to it? If you have trouble erasing the tapes, try the Release Technique (there is a link to their website on mine, www.krystagibson.com). This is a fabulous method for letting go of anything that doesn't serve you and gives actual techniques for getting in touch with your beingness.

Second, name your true self. Choose a dignified, loving, expansive name which you feel really signifies you in the role of high self. Keep the name to yourself, make it a secret not generally shared with others. Call yourself by this name in all your internal dialoguing. See yourself as this person, for indeed you are.

Third, live this image, which means releasing petty, egocentric, power-hungry, self-abnegating behaviors. Be your high self/soul as frequently as possible. Feel yourself as this compassionate, loving, knowledgeable person who is living on the earth plane as whoever it is you are. Make your decisions from this place of knowing rather than only from the level of personality. Spend as much time in the role as you can every day. Yes, it is very easy to forget, it is much easier to slip back into being only one aspect of ourselves. But, with practice, we can be our true, whole selves, more and more frequently.

Does this mean we will no longer face challenges or difficulties in our lives? That we will suddenly sprout wings and fly off into the sunset? No. What it means is that we will be able to face such times from a much larger vantage point within ourselves. It means we will be able to draw upon abilities, knowledge and talents that are currently dormant deep inside us. It means we will be fully functioning, active participants in our own evolutionary process. I think that's something to aim for, don't you?

KYRSTA GIBSON

11
Cycles

If we stop to ponder for a minute, most of us will admit that we see the cycles of nature all around us. They happen smoothly, gracefully, automatically. So much so that we tend to not notice them unless we are being attentive. However, when it comes to our own lives, most of us act as if we are immune to cycles, that we should be able to do whatever we wish and be above any type of cyclical action at all. We're right and we're wrong. It is by learning to be in sync with the cycles or laws of the earth plane that we are enabled to utilize them in such a manner that it looks as if we transcend them.

We've all heard the phrase "timing is everything." I don't agree that it is everything; but, I do believe timing is very important. All else being equal, a project started at one point in a cycle will succeed while if started at another it will fail. But, how do we know which is which? And once we know, how do we align ourselves with the timing so as to make best use of its energy?

The single most important thing I have found in learning about cycles is to set my ego needs aside momentarily and pay attention to what is going on around me and inside me. In other words, forget about what it is we want to accomplish for a moment and watch to see what is already going on. The clues will be magnificent markers to what path might best be tread.

For instance, when I started a newspaper called The New Times in 1985, the metaphysical community was not nearly as large nor as sophisticated as it is today. The first years of the newspaper's existence were very tough financially since I started without capital, bank loans or an investor. I was also beginning something that had not existed before. In other words, I was at the beginning of a cycle with few physical resources.

Although I certainly knew I was at the beginning of something in my life, I still moaned and groaned because it was so difficult and because it felt like I was pushing a large boulder uphill. I was. If I had truly allowed that to sink into my consciousness on all levels, it would not have been as difficult. I made it harder by berating myself and by thinking that because I had a few meta-physical tools in my toolbox, I should be able to do anything easily.

Most parts of the Earth have cold winter seasons. When it is cold outside, it is wise to bundle up in order to stay warm. Do we feel badly about ourselves because we are not able to keep ourselves warm without a coat? Of course we don't. Yet in other parts of our lives we feel bad if we need to adjust ourselves and our schedules to accommodate chilly conditions! I have learned that we can take advantage of cycles, move with them rather than against, and life becomes a lot more fun with considerably less stress. This is the premise from which the "if life gives you lemons, make lemonade" philosophy comes.

Becoming synchronized with life's cycles is, I believe, a long-term project. And sometimes we are better at it than others. After we pay attention and think we know what cycle or cycles we are being influenced by, we can then adjust ourselves to complement them. For instance, if one's business is in a natural slow period we can take advantage of it by moving more slowly our-selves, work with long-term planning, clear out closets or even work fewer hours. This is instead of fretting and worrying, becoming convinced the tele-phone will never ring again because it has been quiet for one day!

If we find our physical cycle is one of needing more sleep than normal, honor the need rather trying to push yourself beyond the limits of what feels comfortable. Go to bed earlier than normal or take a nap mid-day if possible. Become the cycle and find out what it is trying to tell you. If we are tired, there is a reason; we're not just being lazy.

Cycles also have tremendous up periods when everything goes our way, we feel great, life is grand and it seems we can do no wrong. We can enjoy these times, luxuriate in them, feel them all the way down to our bones. They are there to be enjoyed; let's do so.

Have you ever pushed and pushed at something, trying really hard to accomplish some goal and no matter what you did, it just wouldn't go your way? Then out of the blue, everything just worked? Nothing seemed to have changed; it's just that the energy or cycle changed which meant our efforts could bear fruit.

Learning to work with natural cycles teaches the virtue of detachment. When we know that there are seen and unseen forces at work in our lives we can learn to make our plans, do our best to realize them and then let it all go into the cosmic blender knowing that the "right" results will show at the right time. When we are detached from the results of our efforts we cease putting up barriers to our own success. We give the Universe room to work its wonders for us and through us rather than us acting as if we are independent entities calling all of our own shots.

I was told a very simple saying by a Buddhist Master one time. It was the fall of 1985; I had been in business for about four months and was feeling very depressed and distraught over my financial situation. I went to the Buddhist temple just to soak up some of the Master's wonderful energy. At that time he did not speak much English so most of what he said was spoken through a translator. At the beginning of the service I mentally asked him for help. I asked that he say or do something that would help me. During his talk that evening, he looked at me and said, "When you do not have money, remember when you did have money. And when you have money again, remember when you did not have money." You can bet I was pretty astonished!

That saying has stayed with me and I have used it over and over, applying its meaning to various situations in my life. The Master was talking about cycles. There is a natural ebb and flow to all of Earth life. When we are ebbing, it is critical to remember that we will flow again. And when the flow arrives, remember some kind of ebb will appear and plan for it as best we can. If we look back at our lives, we will see that whether we had or did not have at different times in our lives, we were always cared for in some way or another. The saying is also pointing out the issue of trust. No matter whether life is going great or sour, we are loved and cared for in an unlimited and unconditional manner. Remembering this makes all the difference in the world.

We come to the earth plane to learn. We spin our personal wheel of fortune and hop aboard hoping for a thrilling ride in this carnival we call life. We can either get the most out of the rides being offered, even the scary ones like the roller coaster, or we can stand at the gate and complain while we watch everyone else having all the fun.

We can resist the natural cycles of life, swim against the tide and wonder why we never get anywhere or only get there with lots of scrapes and bruises – or, we can align ourselves with the higher forces, relax and allow the currents of change and growth to carry us to our appointed goal. Most of us have chosen the former route for way too long. Maybe it's time for us to lighten up, get in sync with the universe and enjoy ourselves for a change!

12
Karma

*T*he energy of the Universe is spiral in nature, not linear. It is also in constant motion, never static. Every time we act, think or feel we direct the flow of the universal energy and, in some way or another, sooner or later, it will return to us. Because of the constant movement and because this movement is spiral rather than circular, we don't always recognize the return of our own energy. By the time it returns, we are in a bit of a different place than when we sent it out and it, of course, has been modified during the time it has spent traveling.

Some people call this karma while others call it justice. Both of these words usually cause at least mild tension for most of us if not outright fear of retribution. Our learned guilt reactions immediately bring up the ideas of wrong-doing and punishment. We must, however, remember that this law is a neutral one: it does not know the difference between good and bad. It only knows to continue moving. Rather than live in fear of our negative actions, thoughts and feelings returning to us, we can instead focus on the fact that all of our positive ones come back to us as well.

Most people who are consciously and sincerely involved in their spiritual process have moved beyond the more base expressions of humanity such as killing other people, beating or raping, stealing, or committing such acts as physical or sexual child abuse. Anyone who is still engaged in any of these types of behaviors and is also attempting to raise their consciousness needs to understand that ceasing such actions immediately and seeking professional support is mandatory to being able to walk the spiritual path with any measure of success.

For the majority of spiritual seekers, the sort of negative behaviors that are of concern are: judging others, lack of compassion, unkindness, laziness, habits, jealousy, etc. I would like to suggest that, although overcoming these behaviors is certainly an admirable goal that, perhaps, we can use the laws of cause and effect to do so with much less stress and strain than we are perhaps accustomed.

We've all heard the saying "What you give attention to, manifests in your life," and "What you resist, persists." So, if we are giving our focus, our energy, to not wanting something to continue in our lives, what are we doing? We are projecting more of exactly what we say we don't want! By focusing on our own judgmental thoughts and feelings for example, we are simply creating more of the same for ourselves.

What if, instead of giving our judgmentalism more than a passing nod, we placed our thoughts, feelings and actions on the idea of radiating the purest love energy of which we are capable? What would we send out and thus, receive back?

What if, instead of seeing our jealousy as a huge monster breathing down our neck all day we saw it as a mosquito cruising around us looking for a place to land but finding none because we are so busy radiating good will to others?

If, as much as possible, we focus our attention on giving as much love, understanding, peace and compassion to all other beings as we possibly can, our shortcomings and weaknesses won't have time or opportunity to gain enough strength in our consciousness to create havoc in our lives.

Before I get accused of advocating we spend our lives in total denial of whatever issues we need to deal with let me state very clearly that I am not advocating a state of blissful emotional and mental blindness. The Universe refuses to allow that to happen anyway. How many times have you tried to ignore a problem that you simply had to deal with, like it or not? Kept coming back, didn't it? If one tries to use this technique to avoid facing issues such as addictions, deep emotional wounds or pain, cruelty to others, abusive behavior, etc. … it simply won't work. It can't. However, when attempting to heal these sorts of situations, it can certainly help if used in conjunction with appropriate therapies and treatments.

As I understand it, the whole idea behind karma is to help us learn appropriate behaviors for divine humans to engage in. Karma is meant to be a self-correcting mechanism that helps us grow. There is nothing punitive about it. If we want to avoid the karmic repercussions of something we have done or thought, we can do so. All we have to do is take responsibility for our own behavior and learn our lessons.

To accomplish this, the great power of focused attention can be used. How often do you go through your day on automatic pilot, not being really clear about exactly what you did all day? If we can manage to step back from our own lives, even briefly, and take the time to decide exactly how and where we wish to focus our attention and then do so, we will be amazed at the sort of energy return we will experience. The vast majority of us do not intend to hurt other people or ourselves; we usually do so because we either are not paying attention to what we're doing and saying or because we're acting from a place of unhealed pain and suffering.

There is a posture we acquire when we are fully present in our life and paying attention to what we're doing. It is one of balance, peace, centeredness and purpose. From this place we can consciously decide on the movement of our energy and play a large part in what sort of experiences we have in our daily lives.

Many of us are aware of how speeded up time and energy seem to feel these days. The energy we engage seems to return to us much more rapidly than ever before. There is wonderful opportunity in this since it means we receive much faster feedback on how we're doing! This is an ideal time to practice being very aware of what we are thinking, feeling and doing, to try and be as conscious of what energy we're generating as possible.

What we send out, we get back. When we pay attention to what we're doing with our thoughts, our energy, to what we are sending out, we gain an enormous amount of conscious input into how our lives are lived. Even one day spent with greater awareness of what we're doing will reap great rewards.

Many people involved with their spiritual process can mouth the words of how powerful and important we are as human beings, that we are co-creators with the Divine of which we are an expression. Now if we can just begin to actualize this knowing in the everyday practicalities of living we'll begin to see just how true our words really are!

13
Reality

If we want to grow and evolve as conscious spiritual beings, one of the most important things I think we must learn to do is look very, very deeply at everything around us, and in us, so that we can see what is really there.

We spend many years being indoctrinated by whatever culture we are born into. We are taught how life is, all the things we should and should not do, say and think. The process takes quite a bit of time to accomplish but, when completed, another person who runs on automatic has been formed ready to take her or his place with the rest of humankind. Fortunately, we are usually given the opportunity to change our programming if we want to do so.

There are many different ways that people awaken to their spirituality, but in most cases what happens is some sort of seeing through to the other side, to the Spirit side of reality rather than just seeing the physical side. Once this has happened, most people cannot return to their former ways of being or doing. What also happens frequently, though, is that we keep only a slight thread that reaches into the world of Spirit and continue to live our lives as we have in the past. Sometimes we do not question enough; we simply try to slip our spiritual personality on over our programmed one and then wonder why we don't see many changes in our lives!

Exactly what sort of questions can we ask? What in this world can we look more deeply into? And how can we do the asking? What sort of attitude can we hold which will help us do this?

Our attitude can be one of openness, of willingness to see where, perhaps, we have not seen in the past. It can be one of requesting that we be shown truth, the truth about life, the world and about ourselves. I like to imagine myself sitting on top of a small mountain that is covered with flowers, trees, a small lake and lots of friendly creatures. I sit on the ground with my hands in my lap, palms turned upward to signify my openness to Spirit and my willingness to release current attitudes and beliefs. Then I ask away, remaining receptive to whatever concepts, images, thoughts and feelings I may have. I wait with gratitude. And Spirit never disappoints. Sometimes I don't like what I receive or other times I don't understand it right away. But, I always receive some form of communication that deepens my understanding and appreciation of life.

Asking to see how the world and life really are is one of the most profitable exercises we can do. If we begin to see life as it is rather than how it has been presented to us, what a difference this can make in where we choose to invest our energies.

For instance, many of us have been taught that what counts is to get ahead, to have good jobs that pay a lot of money. We have been taught that what material goods we acquire while here determines how well we have done with our lives. To die a pauper is shameful, we have been taught. To die wealthy with lots of houses, cars and money is an honor. Is that really true?

We are born into this world with nothing except a body, mind, emotions, spirit and whatever luggage we choose to bring along from other lifetimes. We have no material goods of our own at all. When we die we take with us exactly the same things… plus, whatever growth in spiritual understanding we have acquired while on earth. I have not seen anyone able to take their material possessions with them when they die, although a few have certainly tried by being buried in their favorite vehicles, etc…

By seeing through this, we grant ourselves tremendous freedom to pursue whatever is truly important to us and our spiritual growth. And maybe that will be the acquiring of material possessions and money. But if it is, we will be doing the acquiring for a higher purpose than simply to go along with what the world says we must do in order to be a success.

Another area we can seek to see clearly about is ourselves. Is it true that we are powerless beings, at the beck and call of anyone perceived to have more power than we do, people such as parents, authority figures, legal structures, bosses and teachers? No, we are not powerless. By entering this society we do agree to certain structures. And in most cases this means we will abide by rules and laws set down before us. But, we do so as a conscious decision to do this rather than because we feel it has been imposed on us from outside.

We can question and ask to be shown about anything and everything in our lives: what is the purpose in being here at this time? What is the truth about our gender and how it fits into the entire scheme of things? What is the truth about our health? Our finances? Our relationships? Our genetic programming?

Once we begin to question, to ask about the true reality of things, we must be willing to see life very differently from before. Like the Hanged One in the tarot we may suddenly find our entire world has gone topsy-turvy. We may discover ourselves viewing life upside down, the exact opposite of how the world at large does. Although this can certainly be upsetting at first, it can also be tremendously comforting since the truth always does comfort – eventually.

Learning to live life with our internal searchlights turned on; penetrating everything we see and experience is actually exhilarating. It gives one a renewed life because we search deeply below the surface and watch the truth reveal itself.

If we wish to call ourselves spiritual seekers, then I think it is imperative that we make every attempt to view and live life from a spiritual perspective, don't you? Do you think it is enough for us to have one foot in the world of Spirit and the rest of our bodies in the world as if we were unawakened? We either want to move along with Spirit or we don't. If we don't, that's fine; then we can place our focus elsewhere. But, if we do, concentrating on seeing the reality behind physical existence can only bring us great joy and peace.

KYRSTA GIBSON

14
Transformations

*D*eath is not a popular topic among most folks; yet, it is something we each face on a daily basis. How we face transitions, transformational experiences, changes – all of which are varied forms of death – tell us a lot about the quality of life we can expect.

A friend of mine recently told me about a T-shirt slogan which he saw being worn by a drug addict in recovery. It said: "Everything I have ever let go of has claw marks on it." How true this is for the vast majority of us. When it is time to change, even when we have asked for the changes, how many of us grasp onto the old with every ounce of strength we can muster? Learning to be a graceful changer or transformer is an art.

Being adept at handling change (which is synonymous with being adept at living one's life since all of life is constant change) means being able to live in an open-handed manner. When we live with our fists clenched tightly around whatever we hold dear, whether this be people, material possessions, activities or ideas, we are living in a manner that promotes distress and pain. It is inevitable that some, if not all, of the things we are clutching so enthusiastically will need to leave us. And when they take their leave by having to force themselves out of our fistedness, be ready for an ouch.

Open-handed living means we cup our hands ever so gently to hold and support what may be dear to us but always leaving lots of space for those things to come and go easily, without our grabbing or clutching them to us. When we release things, people, ideas or even our own physical existence, nothing will have claw marks on it!

Of course, this all sounds great, doesn't it? But, don't we all know how hard it can be to put into daily practice! Sure, we will live easily, openly, generously. Sure, we won't be attached to anything. Certainly, people can come and go in our lives and we will simply allow that movement to occur. Right. Until it happens to be something, someone or some idea which is really important to us and which we feel should be in our lives. Then we hold on with a vise-grip that would make Crazy Glue® look like water.

Living in receptivity to life's changes doesn't mean we won't grieve some of them because we will. And it is important to be as honest as we can with ourselves about how we feel as these changes flow in. Refusing or being unable to express such responses only closes the doorway to successful change even more.

Here are some thoughts that might be helpful in learning how to live with more openness, with our claws in rather than out!

• Change is as natural to our lives as the in and outflowing of the ocean. We can't stop change although we can delay it, usually to our own disadvantage. Once we know that whatever is in our lives right now, including our physical life itself, will someday not be there – then we are ready to accept all changes as a natural process.

• Every ending offers a beginning. Whatever it is that we are letting go of has created the space for something new to arrive. If we don't allow the old to move on, we can't have the new. Can you imagine a snake being so attached to its old skin that it couldn't accept the new one? Or a chick loving its shell so much that it refused to leave?

• Transformation is the reason we are alive. We did not incarnate in order to stagnate. We are here to learn, grow, evolve and change. Fighting the process only makes doing it harder. And we do have to do it, now or later, because it is the nature of the Universe of which we are a part.

• Accessing our soul consciousness as much as possible makes dealing with changes easier because at that level of understanding we are able to perceive more of the big picture of who we are, and why, which makes handling the little ones more joyful.

• Think of the last change you resisted but successfully maneuvered. From the perspective you have today, wasn't it exactly what needed to happen? The next time you find yourself resisting, move into the future and look back with the perspective you will have once the change has been completed.

• If death of the physical body seems scary, remember that we die every night. When the time comes to leave we will have had lots of practice.

This is a time in history when more people than ever want to make changes in their lives. We see vast numbers being willing to enter deeply within themselves and traverse that sometimes dark and frightening region known as the inner self. To do this effectively requires the willingness and the ability to die in many ways and more than once. As each old layer of beliefs about the self is shed, new ones can be born. Doesn't it make sense that learning to be graceful shedders, learning to befriend death rather than to fear it, is to our advantage?

There is a saying that once we have accepted our own death we are free to live. This applies to far more than simply the physical change of moving from the experience of physical embodiment to that of spirit existence. It applies to all of the small deaths we constantly die from moment to moment. When we accept that life is constant change, when we can embrace that life is constant change, we are free to live because we no longer force ourselves to be stagnant pools… we graduate to being forceful, flowing rivers of life itself expressing all the grandeur of which we are capable.

Is there anything in your life that you are trying to hold onto instead of releasing: try opening your hand even if that feels very difficult to do. Let it go. And as you release it, discover the blessedness of lighter living. Learning to not only tolerate change but to actually welcome it, is a most worthwhile project to initiate for ourselves. And part of the beauty is that we will be given plenty of opportunities to practice!

KYRSTA GIBSON

15
Challenges

$\mathcal{A}$re our trials and tribulations a natural part of the life process or do we create them out of negative belief systems? Or are they simply illusions we will someday learn to see through? And do we ever reach a point of development on the earth plane where we no longer have such challenges?

Most of us who are consciously involved in our personal growth and spiritual processes hold a secret hope that someday we'll "get it" and begin to live a challenge-free life. We also don't like to admit this to ourselves, or to other people, and can find all sorts of theories to support our belief!

I will take the risk of critical repercussions and state that I think life on the earth plane is a continuous series of growth cycles followed by tests followed by more growth etc. Our life patterns are similar to the rings that mark the growth on trees. No matter how evolved we become, it is my opinion that we will continue to be faced with challenges of various types and that this is not bad. In fact, it is why we are here! When this process is understood and welcomed rather than avoided, then our lives can be filled with joy, light and laughter like we read about in the books. But it won't be because life offers no hurdles; it will be because we change our attitude towards them.

Unfortunately, when we lose conscious contact with our soul awareness, we also lose sight of why we are expressing as our personality this lifetime. So, we misplace our map and don't always understand where we're headed or why. As soul, however, we are very clear and capable of directing our lives exactly in accordance with our life purpose.

I believe that everything we face in our daily lives is soul-orchestrated and that if we can get in tune with our director we will make beautiful music. As we grow, however, it is necessary for us to undergo some testing and strengthening.

Can you imagine taking some type of coursework and not being tested on the material to see how well we understand it? Would you want people learning how to drive and then not being tested before being let out on the streets? (Watching some folks drive one can wonder how they did pass their test, but at least we know at some point they did!) Would you want to pay to have a house built and then not have it tested or inspected to be sure it met all the codes and ordinances for safety that it should? What about the food you purchase, don't you want it to be tested for purity as well as nutritional value?

We want and expect all these things to be tested and then think that we shouldn't be?

Many of our troubles are simply tests to see how much we have learned and whether or not we are ready for more advanced material. Instead of seeing this, we panic and think we've done something terribly wrong because we face a challenge.

Now, of course, it is also true that some of our challenges come about because we aren't paying attention or because we get sloppy in our thinking or in our choices. We must be willing to face these times as such and not proudly proclaim, "Oh, I'm just being tested so I can move into adeptship… that's why I got fired from my job. Being late and absent 75 percent of the time had nothing to do with it." Sometimes we're being asked to take a look at what life might be like if we were more willing to be responsible for ourselves and our choices.

At other times we aren't being tested so much as we're being strengthened. If we want to grown strong bodies, we think nothing of giving ourselves progressively more difficult exercises to do. We stretch ourselves a little bit further each time we work out. And occasionally we get really enthusiastic and give ourselves huge leaps, truly challenging our muscles and strength.

This also happens at the levels of personal and spiritual growth. Our soul consciousness decides it's time for a huge leap and circumstances are arranged so we can jump. It's no big deal if we fail; it just means we need a bit more exercise before we can accomplish this particular leap. Being unaware of this, we start examining our conscience to see where we have gone wrong. Instead, we would be better advised to put on our sweats and best running shoes, limber up our muscles and get ready to do our best jump!

We have an incredible presence with us at all times, ready and willing to offer guidance and support anytime, any place, under any circumstances. Whether we are trying to develop the virtues of temperance, faith or honesty, our soul consciousness can and will help us. Too frequently we forget to ask. In most instances it would be to our advantage if we could assume a little bit of a more humble posture than is our custom. So often we live as if the personality we are so familiar with is really in charge of our lives. We act as if we are not in need of any sort of more advanced guidance at all. If, instead, we could align ourselves with our own higher consciousness and learn to live through our personalities rather than as them how much happier we would be.

When we face tests, trials, tribulations, problems or challenges using our higher perspective, everything changes. We cease being so immersed in the daily small outcome and view life from the mountaintop seeing the overall perspective that is much grander than we generally are able to conceive. At our own higher level, we will actually learn to welcome our tests and times of strengthening because we will see them for what they are – stepping stones on the path to a state of full self-realization, the true goal of our existence. This does not mean we won't experience such times as difficult or that there will not be pain, because there probably will be. What it does mean is that we will be able to use our experiences for growth rather than staying stuck in the pain.

For myself, I can look back over my life and see a steady progression in the type of tests, challenges and strengthenings I have had. What I see in myself as well as those around me is a refining of the process. The problems have become less frequent and they also consume less of my time from inception to solution. And what I feel when they occur, although potent and intense, moves through me far more quickly than in the past. I can only assume that this process continues in refinement to the point where, like the athlete who seems to jump hurdles so effortlessly, each challenge eventually becomes a welcome chance to stretch my spiritual muscles as I also appear to jump my hurdles effortlessly.

Like a baby human who over the years develops and grows physically and mentally so he or she can crawl, walk and run, so must we mature and ripen emotionally and spiritually. In the process, of course, there will be the falls, the false starts, the dead ends to run into. But, with a conscious awareness of what we are about, we will be able to embrace our earthly existence of joys and sorrows with the same loving attitude with which it is provided for us. Meeting our tests and strengthenings with open arms will serve us well so that we can blossom and bear the fruit of our spiritual labors.

16
Shadows

*M*any of us never thought we would see our country involved in a long-term war again. But here we are. It is frustrating to see the leaders of countries acting like abused adult children who can focus only on power and having their own way rather than being able to step back and make mature adult peace-oriented decisions. It is also frightening since these leaders do, in fact, wield material power over many people's lives.

It is easy for us to sit back and be armchair politicians at this point and to engage in hours of critical judgments about how things ought to be. We can spend a lot of time complaining about the way things are and end up feeling totally helpless in the face of events of such magnitude. Is there anything we can do?

The first obvious answer is, of course, yes. We can visualize world peace; we can pray; we can "send" healing energy and thoughts to the troubled spots of the world as well as to our leaders. But, is there anything else?

Yes, yes, yes! We are part of this planet and we are part of the entire movie that is being shown. Besides taking whatever political actions we deem helpful, we have tremendous power by how we choose to live our lives right now.

How are we contributing to the world situation? If we are living our lives in attack modality we belong in a chair right beside President Bush. If we are quick to go to war with the people around us rather than trying to work things out peacefully, we're prime candidates to be his understudy.

Why do we attack others? Any attacks I have witnessed in my life, or have been a part of, have come from an unhealed place within the self. This is the shadow self, the home of one's inner devil, the place where we store all the ouches of years past, ouches that are just waiting for their chance to strike out at someone else in hopes that this will make them feel better. Of course, it doesn't. One attack always leads to another and another with no resolution in sight. And everyone is hurt, attacker and attackee.

Is there, perhaps, a better way to approach our shadow self rather than just letting it continue to hurt ourselves and others? Yes, there is.

The first step is to admit that we have this self at all. Many, many people within the spiritual community are still unwilling to admit that such a place resides within their personality makeup. They still want to believe that simply because they want a life that is complete love and light one will manifest all be itself. The vast majority of people alive today come from all sorts of abusive backgrounds that set us up for future negative behavior. If we can just allow the possibility that we do have this shadow we are close to being able to start to deal with it.

Second, rather than push this self away, welcome her or him as an important part of ourselves. I don't know many people who can't feel compassion for a small, helpless injured child who needs help. This is what our shadow self is like. It needs our compassion, love, caring and healing – not our condemnation, hate or rejection. Yes, welcoming one's hurt self is not easy. Raising an abused child is not easy. But, it is the task before us if we want to be able to live at peace with this part of ourselves.

Third, there are many books available about healing emotional pain, about dealing with one's injured child within. Start reading them and working with the processes presented.

Fourth, if the work becomes very painful, which is likely, get some help. See a therapist or counselor. Do your best to find one who is ethical and who has done or is doing their own inner healing. Sometimes we can go from the frying pan into the fire if we end up with a person who has not identified or worked with their own issues and who is trying to be a healer. If the first person you see doesn't feel right, go to another. Interview several if you have to, but find someone you feel will support your process and who has the necessary qualifications to help you. At the same time, though, don't be a therapist-hopper, someone who discards a healer every time issues start to be touched.

Find someone good and stick with the program!

Fifth, if you feel an attack coming on, if you feel yourself about to hurt another person, remove yourself from the situation. Go be alone for awhile or call your therapist for a session. Write about how you are feeling. Don't share it with the person you want to attack since sending such written material is an attack. After you get the venom out of your system, burn what you've written.

Sixth, how we think and feel can make a huge difference. When not actively dealing with your shadow self, do your best to think and feel peaceful. I know this can be difficult when in the midst of healing old injuries and maybe one won't be able to do it a lot, but the more peacefulness we can radiate, the more impact we can have on the world situation. Any political actions we decide to take will be enhanced by the state of mind we are in.

Without becoming alarmists or paranoid, this is also a good time to use self-protection techniques that we may know. Because of unrest in the world we are more likely to be around upsetting feelings, thoughts and actions than is normally the case. Also, it frequently happens that the more evolved we become the more we attract denser energies. We don't have to believe that when negativity seems to be camping out on our doorstep we have necessarily attracted it in a negative manner. One of the best protections has been offered by the Bulgarian Master Omraam Mikael Aivanhov. He says that if we are constantly projecting unconditional love nothing can come in our space to harm us. Helena Blavatsky said that a good conscience is the best protection! Then, there's always the circle of white light, calling on the angels, our guides, etc.

Staying out of the way of such energies as much as possible is also a great approach to dealing with them! If someone was throwing a rock at you, you'd duck, wouldn't you? Some metaphysical ducking is called for at times. Burning a candle to keep light before your mind can also help as can using sage and cedar to keep one's own space as clear as possible.

Don't forget to laugh. Maintaining a sense of humor in the face of difficulties goes a long way toward lessening their impact.

Let's be kind to one another, especially right now when the energies are so intense and rough. Let's treat one another as the Gods and Goddesses we truly are. Sometimes this can be hard, especially if we're having to set limits with others and they don't like it – or vice versa. Despite what is going on around us, let's use the principles and ideas we've been mouthing for the past few years. Maybe this is exam time and we're being given a chance to show ourselves how much we've really learned.

This is a rough passage for our country and for the planet. Let's do our part as best we can to contribute to solutions rather than being extenders of the problem.

Note: This was written in mid-2007 when the United States was involved in the war in Iraq, a war instigated by George W. Bush. Hopefully, the political references are no longer true. Of interest is the fact that an earlier version of this chapter was written in the 1990's during the first conflict in Iraq when the elder George Bush was president.

17
Changes

Have your ever noticed how resistant we are to change? And have you noticed that change is the one constant in our lives? Me, too. It's the one sure element in our lives and we resist it! How cleverly human of us.

I wonder why we are this way. Sure, we are creatures of habit and like to have stability in our lives. We seem to be a culture of folks who want a sure thing. Yet at the same time, many of us are interested in growing and evolving. Somehow we must reconcile our desire for stability with the necessity of change if we want to grow.

When we resist flowing with necessary changes we set ourselves up for the electrifying experience of having circumstances changed for us. Like a thunderbolt of lightning, the universe suddenly crashes in upon our lives and says, "Change is needed here. Do it." The result is usually pandemonium accompanied by lots of gnashing of teeth. The changes are thrust upon us and we feel as if we had no choice in the matter. But the truth is, we did.

There is a way of living that enables us to flow with changes rather than suddenly having them forced on us. We can choose whether we'll sit in our mighty towers and wait for the lightning bolt to hit or if we'll climb down into the streets of daily experience and not be a lightning rod waiting to be struck.

When life seems good to us, it is more difficult to be open to changes because we like the way things are now: why change? When life is difficult we tend to hang on to what is for fear that things will get worse. So, what to do? Either way we invite lots of thunder and lightning.

Each of us is here for a specific reason, actually lots of specific reasons. It is up to us to be open to finding out what the reason might be at any given moment and then flowing with it no matter what seems to be required of us. Sometimes the requirements will be pleasurable; other times they will call for hard work we would rather not do.

As the Tao describes it, we can become like water that flows easily and takes the shape of whatever vessel into which it is poured. When water is moving and meets resistance it simply flows around it, over it or, sometimes, through it. If we are like water, we are not pushing or pulling against the natural flow of our lives. Instead, we move with it and even though there will sometimes be rocks, even boulders, in our path, we will simply flow around or over them,

Of course, this all sounds great in theory. It seems a little more challenging when we try to put it into practice and find ourselves screaming the entire way!

I believe it all becomes a lot easier when we allow ourselves to know that this physical existence is not the sum total of who we are or of who the universe is. When we are completely or even primarily aligned with the physical world as if it were all that is, growth and change will seem frightening and unpleasant. Who wants to endure the pains that sometimes accompany changes if one does not believe in a greater purpose than only the one we can see in our day-to-day living?

Being ready to change means living our lives being open to receiving grace. The state of grace as I have experienced it means living life totally open to the higher parts of myself. It means being willing and able to set aside my personal thoughts, feelings and prejudices long enough to receive from the larger part of myself. When we are able to do this, we are, I believe, in the state of grace. We then live life in a grander way. We are able to bypass the pettiness, the small hurts, aches and pains, while remaining open to the larger picture.

Each of us has been blessed with an inner gyroscope which is always showing us which way we need to move or, sometimes, that we need to stand still and catch up with ourselves. It is our connecting link with our destiny and with our guidance. When we live in union with our gyroscope, life flows rather than chuggles along. Even if we are in the midst of great challenges, keeping open contact with this inner leader helps us remain calm and filled with courage. If we can remain open to hearing messages and clucs from this deeper part of ourself, we'll know exactly where we are in relationship to our ability to change at any given moment.

What if we haven't been aware of the areas requiring change, what if we have been out of touch with ourselves, and the lightning bolt strikes? What then… are we doomed to pain and suffering? Not necessarily. Just like stunt workers in the movies, we have to learn how to fall, so we can learn how to handle the lightning flashes should they occur.

In my experience, the best way to respond is willingly and with great flexibility. "So, I wasn't paying attention over here and a big change is needed. I missed that but since I see it now, I'll give it all I've got. What do I need to do?" Then go and do it.

Willingness is probably the single most important factor in being able to move with change gracefully, grace-fully. Even in our darkest hours, if we can sustain an attitude of willingness to change, of willingness to move in the right direction, of willingness to be lead and guided, we find ourselves under the most incredible form of protection possible, that of Divine Guidance. Willingness cannot be taught nor can it be given to another. It is something which must come from deep within a person and which each individual must sustain for her or himself.

Flexibility means we aren't so attached to our own ideas, goals and feelings that we aren't able to move quickly with changes around us. Flexibility gives us the ability to respond quickly and accurately to life's turns in the road.

If we open ourselves to living in the state of grace and then patiently wait, we will find our lives flowing with all the goodness of the universe.

KYRSTA GIBSON

18
Resting

Each of us is the star of our own show. Sometimes we shine and sparkle exuding our inner light while at other times we barely flicker at all. Many assume that working hard and intensely is the secret to shining brightly and, although I agree effort is important, I don't think it is the entire secret.

Our society puts a high value on doing, on performing, on building and expanding. Very little value is placed on resting, playing and rejuvenating. The spiritual community also has a tendency to emphasize output even if it is clothed in less earthly terminology.

Nature teaches us the value of rest and relaxation. Sometimes the most important act we can make on behalf of humanity is to do absolutely nothing, to simply allow our minds, bodies and spirits some time and space to rest and recharge.

I was given a very strong message about this in 1986. I was working seven days a week, 14 or more hours a day with minimal breaks. My life was my business. I lived it and breathed it constantly. It wasn't that I didn't want to play and take some breaks, I just couldn't see how I could do that and still do the job I had been given. The demands at the time were high and I was dedicated to meeting them.

One day I was sitting at my desk working when my entire body began to shake. I couldn't see clearly and I was breathing hard. I was scared, to say the least. I stopped working and allowed myself to go with what I was experiencing, asking for help at the same time. After awhile the shaking stopped and I felt more normal. Over the next few days I moved considerably slower than usual and began to spend some time thinking about what I was doing to myself. I had burned out and unless I made some drastic changes quickly, neither I nor my newspaper The New Times would be able to continue.

It took about a year of slowly making changes in my schedule and of deciding what demands I would and would not meet, but eventually I ended up with a schedule which allowed for free time, for playing, for rest and relaxation. I felt guilty at first for not working constantly. How dare I relax when there was so much work to be done! But, of course, I realized that unless I did take time for myself, no work would be done by me!

To be fair to myself, it is also true that in the early days of that business I did have to put in long hours. Maybe another person could have figured a way to do it without working that much, but for me it was the way I had to do it, if only for the lesson not to do it that way again!

What I learned was that when we give ourselves the room to relax we open ourselves to a much broader picture of what life is all about. It is not just about working. Of course, it also is not just about playing. A balanced approach between the two produces the best results.

A wonderful idea I was given as a prescription at the time is to take an entire day for retreat. This is a day to do nothing, absolutely nothing – no laundry, no housework, no planning, nothing. When I do this, I also try to observe as much silence as I can so I don't even have to make the effort to think clearly enough to speak. I don't give myself an agenda of spiritual exercise either. That can be as much of a distraction from myself as doing the laundry.

What on earth can a person do for an entire day when there is no schedule? Lots of feeling, a bit of thinking and loads of rejuvenating. It can be hard at first if one has been using work or spiritual practices to escape from one's self or one's feelings. Discomfort will start right away; it might even become pretty scary. But if one is willing and able to sit with the discomfort, marvelous breakthroughs can occur.

This is a great time to keep one's journal close at hand to jot down ideas and feelings which might arise. Great material sometimes is given which can be fuel for an entire month of processing!

The first few times I did this I felt guilty. Guilty because I wasn't doing anything. By persisting, however, I learned that I was doing incredible things for myself and others. It's similar to when we begin to engage in meditation on a regular basis. At first we wonder why on earth we're doing this strange thing called meditation. Wouldn't it be better to be out in the world doing something? With continued practice, however, we learn that tremendous growth and development is occurring during this time of supposed inaction. The same is true of retreating from the outer world long enough to get back in touch with one's self.

Allowing ourselves to rest and rejuvenate is one of the highest forms of self-love I can think of. It is also one of the highest forms of other-love. I found that when I was rested and relaxed I was better able to do my job, better able to serve, than when I was running myself ragged.

Resting is also a statement of faith in the universe. We are saying that whatever needs to get done will get done, whether we are personally involved all the time or not. It gives the universe a chance to use channels other than ourselves to do the work which needs to be done. Working long and unreasonable hours is actually a statement of lack because we are saying there isn't enough time for us to do our duties and take care of self also. What a program we are writing with that one!

Part of the goal of living the spiritual life while in the world is to be able to live with our consciousness in both worlds at the same time. We want to be constantly contemplating the wonders of the world of spirit while balancing our checkbook. By giving ourselves time for renewal we make this goal far more likely to be attained because we give ourselves permission to get in touch with the "other world" on a regular basis.

There is a tremendous amount of work to be done these days. The mass consciousness still requires a lot of help to make the breakthrough required for us to have lasting peace on the planet. There can be a temptation to push hard, to work night and day, to feel that if we don't do this, the planet will never evolve to her highest potential. I think it is helpful to remember that none of us works alone, ever. None of us has to bear the entire burden on behalf of the planet or even of our neighborhood.

Not only are there thousands of us working with high dedication on behalf of Mother Earth and our siblings, but we are being assisted by many angels and holy beings who can't usually be seen or heard. It really is okay for us to take our time, to rest and play whenever feasible. What we will find is that when we are rested we can do more work more accurately than when we are tired and grumpy.

Take some time to begin practicing resting. If we simply look around at nature we will see mentors everywhere. The trees and plants, the cats, squirrels and other small animals, find time to take it easy and allow themselves to rejuvenate. Let's allow ourselves to join with the regenerative energies of nature and experience the wondrous sense of being part of a much larger entity than we thought we were.

19
Receptivity

As physical beings our wholeness includes both dark and light They are the same world, however, we see them as opponents to one another and, consequently, treat them in ways that result in pain, lack and many limitations we don't have to endure.

Historically the feminine has been represented by the moon, by the darkness, by the depths, while the masculine has been represented as the sun, the light and the heights. Unfortunately, with these descriptions has also come judgments about which is the best, which is to be given the most respect or honor. As people who have gender, we tend to associate ourselves with one of the two and usually accept the accompanying prejudices.

There are energies on this planet with which we all deal. Energies are at our disposal for everything we do and think. We are comprised of energy and our actions are based on following the energetic impulses we experience.

It is unfortunate that we have assigned gender terms to these different energies because we then tend to relate them to women or men rather than seeing them as energies at everyone's disposal. We cheat ourselves out of some wonderful experiences!

For instance, right now I am drawing on my feminine energies to write this article in the sense that I am being receptive to the impulses of information from a part of myself who has intuitive insights and information. In order to finish the article, however, to be sure punctuation, spelling, etc., are correct, I will draw on my masculine organizing and rational thinking processes. Both kinds of energy are available to me and I use them daily even though I am in a female body.

Although it certainly doesn't always look like it, as a planet we are experiencing a shift from masculine-dominated thinking to having more of the feminine feeling nature mixed in. The only reason this has anything to do with the sexes is because we are divided into two genders on the planet. And until this blending does occur, until the feminine is honored again on planet earth, we will continue to have unequal rights among peoples, men and women, people of color, the differently abled and every other minority group which exists. It is because we do not honor the feminine energies that these inequities exist.

Each of us, no matter our gender, can participate in this liberation of the human species by making some conscious efforts to develop our own feminine natures.

Assuming one, male or female, wishes to develop one's intuitive, receptive, feminine to be more prominent in one's life, what are some of the ways to do so?

The obvious first step is to begin a regular program of internal practices if one is not already doing so. This would include meditation, working with oracular systems such as the tarot and runes, dreamwork, and an increasing openness to the wonders of one's own depths. Spending some daily time simply being receptive without feeling the need to be active helps the process.

The feminine is associated with the moon which represents cycles of growth and development. Attuning ourselves to the cycles of life is a wonderful way to begin or enhance our connection with our inner world. Beginning to follow the moon phases can help one to feel in tune with the earth's processes. Something as simple as deliberately beginning new projects on the new moon and watching them grow and develop as the moon grows to her fullness can begin feelings of connectedness.

Honoring one's feelings, perhaps even learning how to know what we are feeling and then being able to express it appropriately is another feminine blessing long overdue on our planet. We simply do not get a lot of support for having or showing feelings unless they are aggressive or competitive ones. Learning to feel the softer emotions such as loving concern for another, sorrow and grief, laughter and joy will bring us much closer to being balanced individuals.

For many of us allowing ourselves to begin to focus on our feminine selves is a very frightening concept. This is true not only because the feminine is still not valued in our culture but also because we fear what we cannot understand. How many of us really comprehend how intuition, for instance, works? How many of us really know what dreams are? How many of us know why a certain tarot card will turn up exactly when we need to hear its message? These are all aspects of our feminine selves and we simply don't, perhaps never will, understand them.

Our community is about finding and expressing this aspect of our Divine natures, although few people would be willing to put it into these words for fear of alienating those still strongly aligned with mass consciousness. When each of us heals our inner feminine natures, when we allow that part of ourselves to take an equal stand beside our gloriously healed masculine selves, that is when we can begin to enjoy life, to live fully, openly and without feeling bound so exclusively to our rational, linear modalities.

It is true that we take a risk when we decide to plunge into the watery depths of our emotional and intuitive natures. We don't know what we might find. I think it curious that the automatic assumption is that we will find monsters lurking in our darkness. Isn't it also possible we will find splendid creatures of light who like to play hide-and-seek with us? And isn't it possible that the monsters we find might hold exceptional gifts for us in their paws?

People who go inside themselves, deal with and love what they find and then live in touch with their depths tend to have less need to project their monsters onto their neighbors. Given the state of today's evolutionary process, doesn't it make sense that the more people who get in touch with their feminine the greater the chance for lasting peace on earth? So, even though it may not be the most popular game on the planet, yet, wouldn't you agree that it sure seems to be an important one for us to learn how to play?

KYRSTA GIBSON

20
Self-acceptance

In our intense rush to reach enlightenment, many of us frequently miss the most important aspect of living an aware life on the earth plane. We're so busy working to change, fix, elevate, heal, inspire and otherwise alter ourselves that we forget to do the single most important thing: to unconditionally accept ourselves exactly as we are right now.

How many times have you heard that before you can make any effective changes in your life, you must first accept where you are now? Plenty, I'll bet. Me, too. And it's true. It's also true that this is the area most of us spend the least amount of time on. That's why it takes us so long to change!

It seems pretty ridiculous, though, to believe that one must first accept and love unconditionally one's cancer before one can heal it. Or that we must unconditionally accept our material lack before abundance shows up. How can accepting the very thing we don't want lead us to what we want?

The universe simply is. When we accept and love anything in our lives we are accepting and loving what is, the universal life force. When we accept and love the universal life force, we are loving All-That Is. When we are loving All-That-Is, we are at one with it. When we are at one with it we are at one with whatever it is we think we want as well as with what we have now. Sounds complicated, but it isn't. This is probably the simplest spiritual principle ever put forth and the one we have the most difficulty working with because of its very simplicity. Don't we love making things difficult!

When we reject anything or anyone in our lives, we are rejecting the life force expressing itself in that form. It is only when we can accept the life force totally and unconditionally that it can begin to move through us and our affairs to produce all the things we have classified as good and wantable in our lives.

When I think of accepting my life unconditionally, I immediately think of the sun. He shines on absolutely everyone. Can you imagine the sun getting angry at the people in Washington state and saying "I'll withdraw the sunshine from them, I don't like them." (Yes, I know. During our Pacific Northwest winter months it can feel like he has withdrawn his shine and will never show his smiling face again, but he's still there, shining as brightly as ever. We just can't accept as much of it because of atmospheric conditions.)

In principle, this all sounds great, you say. But, how to love unconditionally, accept without strings, all the things in life that we hate so much? How can we accept our pain? Our sorrow? Our darkness? Our weaknesses?

First, realize that the life you are living right now is only one of many. You've been through this before and may go through it again, somewhere, sometime, in some form or another. By realizing this, you begin to take the charge off your life – the charge that says: "I have to get this right, immediately, before this week is over." When you realize you've been at this game a long time and will continue to be, you can remove the sense of urgency usually felt. This will put enough distance between you and your situation so that you can relax.

Second, open your mind to the possibility that what you are experiencing isn't necessarily bad, or at least is not as bad as you would like to believe it is. Can you, even for a moment, imagine that what is happening to you is part of a growth plan engineered by your soul? Can you allow the idea that it might be a wonderful thing that is happening even though it hurts? When someone has been suffering from the pain of cancerous tumors, you can bet it hurts when the surgical procedure is applied. However, don't you think the person is delighted to be free of the tumors once the operation is over? Yes. And this is frequently what is happening with us.

The situations in our lives are there to help us grow. To make us strong, wise compassionate, enduring and capable of bringing forth more Light to the planet. Seen from this perspective, which I admit takes practice and time to accomplish, we will find our entire attitude changes almost immediately. Now, instead of feeling "put upon" or victimized, we feel like master students approaching our coursework with awareness, purpose and integrity.

Third, now that you have some distance from the situation, now that you are relaxed, now that you can accept the possibility that your life situation just might have something good in it, you are ready for the major leap. Try talking to the situation, person, attitude or body condition that is troubling you. Imagine it to be a small child who is doing his or her best with the talents they have been given. Tell it you accept it as a precious and lovable part of yourself. Yes, I said this one was a huge leap. Simply starting this exercise, though, puts you on the road to being there. Talk and act as if you really do love and accept the situation. Get emotional about it. We all know what it feels like to feel passionate love for someone or thing. Conjure up this energy and apply it to your current situation.

Let's pretend to be someone who hates his or her body because it either too large or too small for the standards we hold for correct body size.

Sit quietly and see your body in front of you, appearing as a small child. (The reason I use the idea of imaging your problem as a small child is because that is exactly what it is. Everything in your life is, at least in part, your creation, your "child." You image it that way because that is what it is.) Talk to this child with passion.

"I love you, sweet child of mine. You are wonderful. You are exactly as I have imaged you to be, exactly as I have thought you to be. You are precisely what I have co-created in my life and I love you. I accept you as part of me without conditions, without reservations, without censure or condemnation. I know I have complained about you in the past. I know I have tried to change you through the use of force and violence in my thoughts, words and actions. No more. I accept you and love you exactly as you are now."

Give the child time to respond to you. Watch the expression on her face. As you do this exercise and as you begin to really feel and mean the words you are saying, you will discover that the child's face will begin to smile and be happy. She will no longer be your enemy. You may even discover her asking you how you would like for her to be different in your life! You may find yourself asking the child what she needs from you.

Once we befriend any situation, person or condition, it will begin to work with rather than against us.

Unconditional acceptance of life as it is rather than how we would like it to be, is true magic. It takes us into the realm of the angels who spend their days glorifying the Creator rather than cursing the creation. When we begin to live as the sun, when we accept everyone and everything, we will find an amazing thing happens, effortlessly. As we shine the shimmering light of unconditional love and acceptance on the world around us, it reflects back to us exactly what we have given – unconditional love and acceptance. How could we possibly ask for anything else?

21
Childlikeness

*T*here is a well-known spiritual injunction which says that unless we become as little children we cannot enter the kingdom of "heaven." What does this really mean? Besides working and playing with our inner child at a psychological and healing level, is there something to be learned which can be applied to our spiritual paths as well?

Although our psychological and spiritual lives are not independent from one another, we do have different focuses at various times. For now, I would like to focus on becoming like little children in regard to our spiritual growth without denying the intimate interrelationship between this and our psychological selves.

What qualities of the child can we integrate into our lives that will assist our continued spiritual progress?

First would be the quality of openness. When we were little children we were so incredibly open to other people, to life, to ideas. We had to be. We were starting from a place of nothing and had to learn how to do just about everything. Our ability to learn was greatly facilitated by our capacity to be open. Is that still true of us today?

How do we respond to new information? Do we stand back from it and take a very cautious, almost cynical attitude, like a grown-up would? Or do we enthusiastically embrace new ideas and information and try them out? Children have a natural curiosity and interest in just about everything. They don't accept everything they are told or shown, but they usually exhibit interest, and experiment with the new before rejecting it.

On the spiritual path we can be either open or closed. If we allow ourselves to close down, we cheat ourselves of wonderful opportunities to grow and to learn. And we definitely miss out on some very interesting experiences.

When presented with new ideas, be the child. Be open, be interested, be willing to take the position that there could be something exciting for you in whatever it is you are facing. The Zen teachings call this having "beginner's mind." When we are new to any endeavor we have a natural attitude of being learners and we tend to be open to new information and experiences. When we begin to see ourselves as experts, however, we close ourselves to new information. Who can teach an expert anything?

Another quality children have that we could incorporate is innocence. By the time we are adults, most of us are burdened with large amounts of guilt. Many of us spend lots of time and money in therapy learning how to release our inappropriate feelings of guilt and responsibility for other people's behavior. We are innocent and when we can allow ourselves to approach our spiritual process with natural child-like innocence we find ourselves showered with ideas, inspiration, and feelings that are very angelic. Being a spiritual child is like being an angel. We exist simply to be whomever we are however we are led to do that – without judgments, incriminations or other gunky attitudes coming between us and our Divine Source.

Becoming like a little child spiritually is about letting ourselves be free again. Free to explore, to learn, to experience life and everything it has to offer. How often have you seen people dismiss the actions of a child, just because he or she is a child. Children and a childlike attitude can get away with a lot. We don't expect stoic adult attitudes from children and shouldn't expect it from our spiritual selves either.

Being a child means learning how to loosen up and laugh again. How many of us remember what it is like to giggle? When was the last time you laughed so hard you cried? Approaching life with humor lightens it up a lot. Have you ever watched a group of children at play? They laugh for no reason at all. They become what most adults would call "silly." We really have placed a heavy judgment on being silly as if there is something wrong with it.

There is a lot to laugh at in the world, especially once we enter the spiritual realm. Contrary to what we have been taught by orthodox religion, God/dess enjoys laughing – immensely. Look at all the funny things here on earth! Someone once said that the sacred name of God is laughter. That's why no one can pronounce it!

When we approach our lives with openness, innocence and giggles, the entire process changes, almost magically. Instead of spirituality being a serious, morose sort of business that requires great strain and concentration from us, it becomes a living of our lives easily, effortlessly, with joy and happiness. What about the darkness and the bad times. Yes, they exist. Have you ever seen a child fall down and hurt themselves? They cry and scream and scrunch up their faces something fierce. One would think the world was ending. When I've seen this happen I thought the child had seriously hurt herself. Almost as suddenly as the crying starts, it stops and the child begins to explore and play again.

On our journeys we will be faced with darkness, with difficulties, with hard times. When this happens, the best thing for us to do is be the child and get into it. Whatever our darkness is, let's jump in with both feet, fully experience it, be it, scream it, do whatever the moment requires. When we do this, we will discover that the darkness passes and daylight comes again. Just like what happens every 24 hours. No matter what kind of darkness we encounter, eventually we will always experience the light and vice-versa.

I recently had a very poignant example of this. On my drive to work one morning I came across two dogs in the middle of a country road. I had seen them playing in the past and knew they were pals. One of them was dying in the middle of the road. He had just been hit by a car that did not stop to render aid. His back was broken and I knew he would not live long enough to reach a veterinarian. His pal stood over him in grief. I was immediately thrown into a state of tremendous sorrow, confusion and horror. I stood there feeling totally helpless on the physical level while the dog took his last few breaths. I then moved the broken body to the side of the road so he wouldn't be hit again and so his owners could find him when they returned home. Then I comforted his friend briefly and continued to work, changed by my totally unexpected encounter with the darkness of the incident. I allowed myself to grieve, to cry, to feel the reality of what had just occurred. I spent the day with mourning as a backdrop to everything I did.

The next day some unusually wonderful things happened for me. Without bogging down in the metaphysics of the incidents which occurred (and which are very profound in a positive way), what happened was my being given an opportunity to experience the light and the dark in close proximity to one another. I was given a chance to live my life, feel my feelings, just be who I was in the situations presented without needing to judge or analyze them. I was given a chance to be the child, to stretch from intense sorrow to exuberant joy in a brief period of time and know each for what it is.

It can be a challenge to maintain a childlike attitude in today's world because there seems to be so many serious things happening all of the time, Although children can be serious when necessary as should we, they have an ability to flow through and with events that most of us have lost. Becoming a spiritual child again puts us back into the flow of life, whether what we are dealing with is serious or light. Whether we are walking in a beautiful park, enjoying the flowers, squirrels and birds or in the middle of a business trans-action, we can be experiencing life from a place of spiritual childhood. We can remain open, innocent and playful no matter the circumstances in which we find ourselves.

How do we accomplish this? By reminding ourselves at least a few times daily that, in truth, we *are* children. We are children of the cosmic Mother and Father. We have been placed in the wondrous garden called Earth so we can explore and experience its many treasures. Our Cosmic parents are not abusive like so many of our parents were. The cosmic mommy and daddy don't expect us to grown up over night and be responsible for *them*! They simply want us to be who we are and live our lives as fully as we can.

We can listen to the call of our dysfunctional planet and its method of living life or we can, instead, learn how to hear the celestial sounds inviting us to be the divine children we really are, We can either approach our experience with lots of glumness and dread, expecting the worst at every turn (and getting it!), or we can cultivate our long forgotten ability to be children and just live our lives with large amounts of gusto and appreciation!

22
Limitations

*A*s it possible for us to let go of our limitations as we are so frequently encouraged to do? Can we really "have it all?" Can we learn how to create circumstances and conditions in our lives so that pain is foreign to us, so that everything is always exactly the way we want it to be? Can we have health, wealth, right relationships and beauty at all times?

I've always interpreted "let go of your limitations" to mean that someday I would have no limitations, that I could be a limitless person with nothing holding me back from being all that I can. Lately, though, I've started to gain a new understanding of what letting go of my limitations might mean on a functional rather than philosophical level.

To "have it all" in the true sense means to become fully functioning whole beings: to reach deeply inside ourselves and pull out into the physical world a counterpart of our inner selves. Sometimes the problems, limitations and situations we have in our lives make this process feel like pulling taffy, but in truth these are the methods we have been given to accomplish our goal.

Think about the times in your life that have been the toughest, the hardest. Weren't these also the times you grew the most, deepened your understanding the most? Weren't the limitations you were working through exactly what helped you to grow so that you could express more of your real self on a daily basis?

Depending on where we are in our evolutionary process, we can have lots of money or little. We can have beautiful material objects to enjoy or we can be without much at all. What we have in the outside world is not a complete expression of who we are in spirit. If each of us could express as we are in spirit, then indeed we would have it all because we are limitless beings at the level of spirit. When we come into incarnation, however, we deliberately limit ourselves in order to create, to grow to experience life on the earth plane.

So, does this mean we should stop trying to create nice things for ourselves? Should we stop the visualizations, the affirmations, and take life as it comes, kind of like a jellyfish who just seems to float along with the tides?

No, if we get in touch with our greater selves, our higher selves, our soul consciousness, we will be shown through our desires and attractions what things, people and events we need to have in our lives. Those are then the ones we set about bringing into physical form. The limitations, pressures, and challenges that arise along the way are the stuff from which we create the end results. It is through our limitations that we expand who we are.

I am beginning to get a glimmer that what is actually meant about letting go of our limitations is that we are not to worry about them or invest them with power they do not have. In other words, so what if someone is not as intelligent as she would like to be? So what if their physical appearance isn't what some folks tell them it should be? So what if we weren't born into a wealthy family and we have to work hard for every penny we earn? So what?

I have found it helpful to learn how to dance with my limitations rather than to curse them or try to chastise myself for having them. Dancing with my limitations means contacting them in a deep way and finding out why they exist. What are they trying to teach me about myself, about life? What way are they encouraging me to grow and become a more complete person? I have found it much easier to let go of limitations after I understand and embrace them than when I fight to keep them.

Here are some ideas for dealing with limited areas in your life.

First, accept the limitation as a temporary structure that can help you. Consider it a friend rather than a foe. This is more easily accomplished if you bring to mind some other difficult times you had and remember how they turned out. I know that accepting one's limitations is frequently quite a challenge and is not easily accomplished in many cases. But, I also know that miracles are birthed when we take the plunge and accept ourselves as we are.

Second, ask it what it wants to do for you. What is it trying to teach you? How does it want you to change? What does it want you to do? Spend some time on this one because it holds the key to your eventual ability to let go of the limitation.

Third, once you know the reason for the limitation, help it meet its purpose. Find books, tapes, a counselor; whatever way or ways you can think of to learn or experience whatever the limitation is there for. Rather than push against it, rather than trying to make it go away, help it accomplish its end.

Fourth, be grateful. No matter what is happening in your life, be grateful. Thank the limitation. Thank yourself for attracting the limitation. Be grateful and watch to see the changes in your life immediately. Gratitude always brings great positive changes.

Fifth, after doing all of the above, forget about your problems and go have some fun. Play games, take a walk, smell the flowers. Go do something totally uninvolved with your limitation. Just forget about it for awhile and let your deeper mind, your soul, deal with it. Let it all go and have a good time.

We can either stew about our challenges and limitations or we can embrace them and live life fully, not denying any aspects of who we are. Life in this world is so much richer when we decide to engage all of it rather than enjoy the parts we find immediately attractive. Letting go of limitations, stating "so what" and then going ahead enthusiastically, gives the freedom we all seek. But the secret is that we can have our freedom right now, today. We don't have to conquer our limitations to be free of them. All we have to do is dance with them.

KYRSTA GIBSON

Appendix

22 Steps to a Success
Your Guide to a Fulfilling Life
by Krysta Gibson

$\mathcal{T}$his is a shortened version of the 22 steps. Use these when you want a quick refresher of each message or you don't have time to read the entire chapter.

• Whether a person is beginning their day, a new venture, or relationship, it is a time of excitement, freshness, unknown factors, risk-taking, and the expenditure of a lot of energy. When we start something, we end something else so every beginning is an ending. When you start something, realize you are jumping off a cliff. You are taking a risk. And….you will be just fine, no matter what happens. Relax and enjoy the process.

• When trying to manifest a "success" of some kind, remember that you are a channel for energy rather than the originator of the energy. Your job is to direct the flow of the energy in the direction of your choosing. To do this: use your mind, choose your thoughts carefully, focus on what you want and not on what you do not want because what you focus on will be what you manifest. Use your will to keep going when the days get long and tough. Use your emotions to create an atmosphere of success. Remember a time when you were successful in the past and then use that energy to act "as if" you are already succeeding.

• Use the power of your subconscious to help you: use visualization, affirmations, self-hypnosis, etc. At the same time, watch your words, your actions, your thinking, and your environment so that you are not contradicting yourself all day long!

• Align with your natural creative abundance by doing something fun and creative every day to keep your juices flowing: set aside time to write a poem, draw a picture, sew something, color in a coloring book, sing, write, bake bread! When the Universe sees we're willing to be receptive to our creativity, the ideas and feelings will continue to flow smoothly.

• A well-ordered life is usually more peaceful and harmonious than one that is cluttered or in disarray. To have order, ask yourself, "What am I trying to accomplish? Is my life structured to support what I want or will it sabotage my efforts? Be willing to change the goal or the structure if they don't match up. A well-ordered emotional life is also conducive to an overall successful life. If there are emotional issues requiring your attention, take care of them.

• Get in touch with and follow your inner guidance. Tuning in to our inner Wise One requires receptivity, discernment, trust, solitude, silence, commitment, and the willingness to experiment and to take risks. We must spend quiet time in order to hear this voice. It won't shout but it does whisper and if we are too busy in the outer world all of the time we won't hear it.

• Whatever you do, do it with love. In order to love what you do you must love yourself and those around you. If you are not able to love what you are doing, it is time to consider a change. Life is too short to spend your time and energy doing something that bores or annoys you. How can you uplift the planet when you are walking knee-high in mud?

• Pay attention to what you say. Sloppy thoughts lead to sloppy words. The more we hone our ability to focus thought for creative purposes, the faster and more clearly our thoughts and words will produce results. Because our words are filled with creative power, this means we can influence our growth by the words we speak and the ones we choose not to speak. Words give great power to our thoughts.

• It takes tremendous courage to follow one's vision regardless of the consequences. Courage evidences itself through persistence, concentrated efforts, faith, joyful risk-taking, and a relaxed sense of humor about it all. It is easy for us to confuse being strong with being overbearing, pushy, and ruthless. A test most of us are given is that of being willing to persist with a course of action when things seem not to be working or when the going gets tough. Many of us give up way too soon in whatever we're doing and then bemoan the fact that our project didn't work out. When we are willing to be persistent, are operating from a deep faith in life itself, and are willing and able to request help as the need arises, taking risks becomes a much more joyful prospect.

• Whatever situation you find yourself in, you have been led there by your inner self, the self who sees your life from a higher perspective. We are multi-faceted beings and true success happens when we are able to consciously merge our everyday understandings with this inner self who is guiding our ship. When we allow our soul-self to actively influence us, when we welcome it consciously into our lives, hold on, because all sorts of miracles will begin to happen for you.

• There are natural cycles to life and this includes everything: home life, work, relationships, money, creativity – all of it. The cycles in nature are easy to see and we are able to accept those fairly well most of the time. For some reason, though, we seem to think that our lives should be in the harvest cycle all the time. What about planting, watering, digging out weeds and the little plants that don't make it because of the heat or the cold? Just like nature, our lives have cycles. The wise person pays attention to the cycle of their life and acts accordingly. If things are moving slowly, don't panic. Use this time for planning, more networking, and to rest when you can. Learning to work with natural cycles teaches the virtue of detachment. There are seen and unseen forces at work in our lives. We can learn to make our plans, do our best to realize them, and then let it all go into the cosmic blender knowing that the "right" results will show up at the right time. When we are detached from the results of our efforts we cease putting up barriers to our own success.

• What we give our attention to is what we get more of in our lives. How much time do you spend fretting or worrying about your life? How much time do you spend thinking about how successful you are and will continue to be? What we send out into the world is what we get back from it. If, as much as possible, we focus our attention on giving as much love, compassion, understanding, and peace to all other beings as we possibly can, our short-comings and weaknesses won't have time or opportunity to gain enough strength in our consciousness to create havoc with our lives. I am not talking about burying your head in the sand. I am talking about using the power of focused attention to attain balance, peace, centeredness and purpose in your life.

• Release! Set your goals, have your vision, make your plans, go to work, do your best…then let it all go into the Universe. It is true that we must be very active in our lives and tend our dreams with great care and love. What is also true is after doing that we need to let it all go. We view our lives with a somewhat limited viewpoint. There is so much going on beneath the surface at any given time, things we don't see and don't sense. When we let it all go and allow the Universe to do its part, we open the door to a much greater level of success than we ever thought possible.

• Be open to changes in your life. Change is as natural to our lives as the in and out flowing of the ocean. We can't stop change from happening, though we can delay it by resisting it, usually to our own disadvantage. Your dream or project is a living entity and as such it is subject to ongoing growth and change. As its steward, your job is to be in touch with the soul of what you are doing and to be ready to respond to the changes it wants you to make.

• Tests, challenges, and strengthening are a natural part of the life environment. Because you are approaching your life with a spiritual base and as part of your spiritual journey, you can be assured that you will meet many tests and challenges along the way. Some people think that because they are involved in a spiritually-oriented task, things will be easier for them. Not so! Whatever you are doing is part of your path; you need to be open to the difficult times and embrace them. Everything that happens in your life is a gift. How you receive it and what you do with it paves the way for your future.

• Keep your sense of humor! Oh, my, but we do tend to get so serious about everything. After all, we are about such lofty things as enlightenment, healing, and world peace! Truly, the lighter we can be, the more we allow ourselves to laugh and see the humor in our daily path, the happier and more successful we will be. The Universe loves a good laugh – just look around you at the different animals, plants, and humans that exist (including yourself)!

• Be willing to live from the state of Grace. What does this mean? We are blessed with an inner gyroscope that is always showing us which way we need to move or, sometimes, that we need to stay still and catch up with ourselves. It is the connecting link with our destiny and with our own guidance. Start your day in the state of Grace with meditation and prayer. Then stay aligned with this deeper inner you and watch how easily your day flows.

• Rest and play when you can. Sometimes we are so serious because we see our dreams as such an important part of the changing of the planet that we forget to take time for ourselves. It is so important to rejuvenate ourselves by taking time to simply be. Take an entire day to do nothing. Yes, that is difficult to do, but the results are tremendous!

• Balance your feminine and masculine selves. Going after a goal or dream draws greatly on our active masculine energies. Remember to tend to the feminine self, the one who is intuitive, emotional, and mysterious. A successful person is able to draw upon both sides of their nature – without feeling one is more important than the other. We can't have light without dark. Our days are balanced and so can we be.

• Love your life exactly as it is right now. Maybe it is not performing up to your expectations yet. Love it anyway. Until you love and accept your life how it is, you will never be able to shepherd it to the place you want it to be. Unconditional acceptance of our lives as they are - rather than how we want them to be - is true magic. Doing this allows us to be like the sun that shines on everyone, good and bad alike. When we live this way – when we accept everyone and everything as it is now – we will find an amazing thing happens effortlessly. As we shine the shimmering light of unconditional love and acceptance on the world around us, it reflects back to us exactly what we have given – unconditional love and acceptance which is the basis for a very successful life!

• Allow yourself to be childlike. Approach your day with the openness, innocence, and freedom of a child. Yes, I know this may seem strange because how many children can lead an adult life effectively? What I am talking about is a basic attitude that underlies the adult self who has to make the critical decisions of the business day. Being childlike with your day means allowing yourself the room to lighten up and to remember that you have a cosmic mom and dad who are really in charge of everything. Keeping that in the back of your mind allows you to be more playful which means you will attract higher and more refined energies to your day.

• Dance with your limitations! We all face a variety of limitations of one kind or another. Even though we are unlimited beings, we do live in a world with physical limits. We have a choice: either cry and stomp our feet and fight our limitations, whatever they are, or dance with our limitations, get to know them, ask them out for dinner! Find out why your limitations are with you and what it is they want to teach you. Letting go of limitations, stating "so what" and then going ahead enthusiastically gives us all the freedom we seek. The secret is that we can have our freedom and success right now, today. We don't have to conquer our limitations to be free of them. All we have to do is dance with them!